George's Kaddish for Kovno and the Six Million

Catherine Gong

Edited by Michael Berenbaum

To order additional copies of this book, contact:
Xlibris Corporation
1-888-795-4274
www.Xlibris.com
Orders@Xlibris.com
51241

Reviews for "George's Kaddish for Kovno and the Six Million"

Catherine Gong has written a powerful and passionate work about her encounter first with the work and later with the Kovno ghetto photographer Hirsch Kadushin. The result is a deeply satisfying book that has made her the witness of the witness. Kadushin understood to document for eternity what he was experiencing in Kovno with the one tool that he had, a clandestine camera. His pictures are personal; they show Jews in their ordinary life and are indispensible to understanding their plight. Unlike most perpetrator photographs that dehumanize the victims, these photographs rehumanize them and Gong has beautifully described their impact on a young Asian-American woman who found these as her pathway in the abyss. It is a gripping work that depicts both the Shoah and the world that we live in.

—**Michael Berenbaum, United States Holocaust Memorial Museum, Former Project Director; Survivors of the Shoah Visual History Foundation, Former President; Professor of Jewish Studies, American Jewish University; author of "The World Must Know"**

Catherine Gong's tribute to the Lithuanian Holocaust survivor George Kaddish (Zvi Hirsch Kadushin) includes the photos he took in the ghetto of Kovno during the occupation by the Germans in the 1940s at great risk. It's an astonishing story that Ms. Gong has unearthed as we can see from the pictures that speak with a terrible eloquence of the near-unbelievable lives of the Kovno Jews. Catherine Gong reached George Kaddish in Florida shortly before his death and has rescued his story and his photos from obscurity in her memorable tribute to this heroic Holocaust survivor.

—**Stanley Poss, Ph.D., Professor of English, Emeritus, California State University Fresno**

One of the most powerful forms of Holocaust resistance was the enormous struggle to maintain personal dignity and human kindness. In the darkness of the Kovno ghetto, George Kaddish took clandestine photographs to celebrate his doomed neighbors and condemn the atrocities of their tormentors. These photos are at once disturbing yet life-affirming, repellent yet deeply moving; their publication alone is a minor triumph. In unearthing this lost chronicle, Catherine Gong has accomplished a remarkable work of both scholarship and service. She has remembered the rememberer, and said a prayer for the man whose life itself was a prayer for the six million.

—Zac Unger,
Brown University;
Firefighter,
Oakland Fire Department;
author of "Working Fire: The Making of an Accidental Fireman"

Contents

For George Kaddish who gives us much to learn, to
Yehuda Zupowitz who sacrificed everything for us to see, and
for Solly who gives George's images a kindred voice.

Acknowledgements

Holocaust history has always gripped me. It teaches that the strength of the human spirit is unrelenting. My family and friends have also held me tight throughout my process of learning, doubting, believing, and finally completing. Now, it is with utmost humility that I offer my thanks to those who helped me with my book.

I thank Rabbi Abraham Cooper at the Simon Wiesenthal Center and Museum of Tolerance for preserving a dear man's legacy and appreciate the assistance of Caroline Waddell at the United States Holocaust Memorial Museum and Zippi Rosenne and Aviva Heller of Beth Hatefutsoth. I thank George Birman for introducing me to a great man and Pola Birman for her hospitality. I thank Professor Jill Shapiro and Professor Diana Bowstead of Columbia University for their inspiration and patience. I am especially grateful for Betty Guttmann who not only gave me syntax and pointers but kindness. Betty's enthusiasm, energy, and our love of chocolate pulled me through. I am grateful to Michael Berenbaum who remembers my long mourning and whose work, *The World Must Know* gave me the encouragement to open every book and turn every page during my research. And I am very thankful for Solly Ganor's published memoir, *Light One Candle*. Mr. Ganor's words communicate, with kindred eloquence, the horrors of both the Kovno ghetto and the Holocaust.

Naturally, I associated the acts of studying, recording, and discovering with this project but when intimidation and fear came unexpectedly, Professor John Felstiner of Stanford University pushed me out of my many hiding places where I cowered, stammered, and shivered. Whether I was writing on the west or east coast, Professor Felstiner's spoken and written words dried my eyes and wiped my face. With every scrape, bump, and bruise, Professor Felstiner bandaged me and stood me up. Despite his long-standing preference for me to address him by his first name, I can never think of him as "John" but will forever think of him as teacher.

For spiritual guidance, I thank Mrs. Annette Lantos. I met Annette while working for her husband, Congressman Tom Lantos, who served California's

12th District before he passed away. Even though I primarily worked for him and his staff, I also became the recipient of Annette's wisdom. Annette's elemental, yet magical way of looking at our world will be with me forever. Despite being a Holocaust survivor, Annette never identified herself with victimization. On the contrary, Annette teamed up with her husband, Tom (who was also a survivor) and championed human rights for all. Annette's steely determination matched her husband's and her actions impacted Capitol Hill and the world. Witnessing and recalling Annette's contributions inspired me throughout this project when I doubted myself.

This journey required basic provisions and I have many to thank for my necessities. I've survived in D.C. under the watchful eye of Dean Heyl. I thank Rudolf Rohonyi for his warm kitchen and extend deep gratitude to the Alexandria City firefighters at Engine Co. #201 for feeding me. I was nourished with their hearty food and most importantly, their many stories of mayhem and close calls. Their narratives were chock-full of humor and their laughter and silliness helped me navigate through the unspeakable grimness of Holocaust testimonies. I especially thank Captain Anthony Casalena's reflexive nature to assist me and care for my heart. And lastly, I thank my father and mother, James and Hazel Gong; and my brother, Michael. I am the product of my family's sacrifice.

Catherine Gong
Alexandria, Virginia
12 September 08

A Prefatory Note

Over the years, survivors, family, and friends have contributed their knowledge to the United States Holocaust Memorial Museum to provide the names of the people and places George Kaddish photographed. Since these individuals came from different areas of eastern Europe, very often, the same person's name was spelled differently, or depending on their relationship, many contributors referred to some of George's subjects by a nickname or in an informal way.

When I first started writing, my reflex was to impose a consistent spelling for each person's name throughout the photo captions, diary, and testimonies I reference in my book but my approach soon changed. By imposing one way of spelling a person's name, I would be taking away the "voice" from the other people who knew George's subjects. Also, it would suggest that I preferred one person's pronunciation or spelling over another. Because of these concerns, I've recorded all the names in my book exactly as it was written by those who have witnessed.

My choice to use all the variations of a person's name, as it was written, may be confusing. I do apologize for this but to minimize confusion, I've compiled a small, informal list of people mentioned in my book, along with the other names they are known by:

> "Alexander" is also recorded as "Shaya," "Abrasha," and "Avrasha."
> "Bergman" is also recorded as "Bregman."
> "Elchanan" is also recorded as "Elkhanan."
> "Gladshstein" is also recorded as "Gladstein."
> "Hoffmekler" is also recorded as "Hofmekler."
> "Kaddish" and "Kadish" are also recorded as "Kadushin."
> "Michael" is also recorded as "Misha."
> "Stupel" is also recorded as "Stupfel."

"Yankale" is also recorded as "Yankele."
"Yehuda" is also recorded as "Yudel."
"Yehudit" is also recorded as "Jehudit," "Judith," or "Dita."
"Yitzhak" is also recorded as "Isaac."

All featured dialogue and recollections are recorded to the best of my ability. Any errors are unintentional.

—C

An Unexpected Search

Wanting to learn more about the Holocaust, I went to the campus bookstore after class. Under the "Holocaust," "European History," and "WWII" sections, there were dozens and dozens of titles and my fingers picked one book randomly. While in my hands, this book fell open to a page and my eyes settled on a name, "George Kaddish." What preceded this was "Hirsch Kadushin," the man's birth name. Why would anyone rename himself after the Kaddish, the Jewish death prayer? And did his last name have anything to do with the Holocaust?

Little did I know that my initial interest about George Kaddish's last name would draw me into a visual world of unimaginable suffering and survival. In this world I met a man who linked his entire identity to bearing witness during and after the Holocaust. But more importantly, my curiosity about George's last name would help me better understand the possibilities of healing and renewal after the Holocaust.

But there in the campus bookstore, I knew none of this and hardly anything about the Kaddish prayer. Jews recited it after the death of a loved one. Besides this, I knew nothing else. Again, why would a person change his name from Kadushin to Kaddish? I looked at the book again and upon reading further I learned that George Kaddish took pictures of Nazi atrocities with a hidden camera. The reprinted photo that was his in this book had the caption: *A neighbor of Hirsch Kadushin (George Kaddish) was murdered by the Lithuanians with his family. As he lay dying, [the neighbor] wrote with his own blood on the kitchen floor "Yiddin Nekamah," "Jews Revenge."* (1).

The translated Hebrew was inside the caption of George Kaddish's black and white photo. The floor looked dirty but the written characters spelling out revenge were clear. I imagined Kaddish's response to the floor's message before he photographed it; a discovered and glistening red horror. But whether it was black and white or in color, a phrase written in human blood was too much for me to fully process and I looked away. How was George Kaddish able to calmly record the evil deeds of the Nazis? Besides this one photograph, there were only a few more lines about Kaddish. Naturally, I had more questions. How many pictures did he take? Were Kaddish's other photos as grim as this one? And again, why did the photographer's spelling of his last name resemble the Kaddish prayer? Did this man identify himself with Judaism or death itself?

"On the night of June 25-26, 1941, one day after the German occupation of Kovno, Lithuanian nationalists unleashed a massive . . . pogrom . . . Over eight hundred Jews were murdered in their homes in the most savage manner . . ." Date: June 26, 1941. Locale: Kovno Ghetto. Photographer: George Kadish/Kadushin. Photo Credit: USHMM, Courtesy of George Kaddish/Zvi Kadushin.

Within minutes I bought the book, left the campus bookstore, and went to the library to find anything I could about George Kaddish. I didn't know much about the Holocaust but knew that recording Nazi activities was punishable by death. I went through the library stacks. I had to find something, anything with 'George Kaddish' or 'Zvi Hirsch Kadushin' in it. Of course, there were many entries under the 'Judaism' and 'religion' sections of the library and countless entries about the Kaddish death prayer itself but there was nothing about a man taking pictures during the Holocaust. Stanford University's Green Library wasn't exactly small and I grumbled through the dimly lit shelves. If Stanford didn't have any information about George Kaddish, maybe no library would. I left campus and drove to the Jewish Community Center's library. I had always driven by it but never went in. I checked the database and again, numerous titles about religion and the Kaddish prayer but nothing on Kaddish the man. I asked the Center's librarian about George Kaddish. He wasn't familiar with his name or work during the Holocaust and he pointed me in the direction of San Francisco State. While I was there, I did find a ten-sentence article in German. I recognized some of the obvious words, such as 'foto' and 'konzentration kamp' but this obviously was not enough.

Resignedly, I returned to the Jewish Community Center to find something about the Kaddish prayer. If I couldn't find anything written about the photographer's courageous activities during the Holocaust, maybe I would know more about Kaddish the man by familiarizing myself with the Kaddish prayer. Was he a secular person or a devout Jew? I felt unprepared. I knew nothing about Judaism and very little about religion. My thoughts took me back to when I wore knee socks. I envied my classmates who went to church. During recess, my friends would sometimes complain about Sunday school, reading the Bible, and singing. After school and on the weekends I worked at my family's grocery store and on Sunday mornings I wondered what my classmates were learning.

I'm a Chinese-American and daughter of a first-generation father and second-generation mother. Stories from China, the old country, haunted me. My grandmother once lived in a house with dirt floors and I had a grandfather who was mistaken for dead at birth. In grandfather's village, there was no cemetery or burial ground. Simply, grandfather was placed in a pile with other refuse and awaited disposal before a shocked neighbor discovered grandfather alive. The importance of valuing every grain of rice is still with me. Although my family's misfortunes occurred in another land, the reverberations of these experiences were still felt in America and continue to resonate inside me. For instance, expressing one's thoughts was not encouraged in my family's household. Discussing politics and religion were considered activities for trouble-makers and avoided altogether; "The tall tree gets crushed by the wind" is an old proverb summing up my childhood. (2). Even though I was born in California, the concept of the freedom of speech for my elders seemed to be a foreign one; a concept that could not silence their memories of oppression and sorrow. Therefore, my ears pricked up when someone freely spoke about baptism, Sunday school, or just being an altar boy at recess. When my father drove by the two churches on the way to our family's grocery store, I imagined what magic took place behind those stained-glass windows and sturdy, oak doors. If I only knew more about Catholicism, Protestantism, or just some general knowledge about religion, maybe I would have some idea of what the Kaddish prayer was and why this photographer renamed himself after it.

Regret and self-admitted ignorance however didn't impede my curiosity and at the Jewish Community Center I sorted through books about theology, Talmudic law, and the five books of Moses. Finally, I brought two books up to the counter and the librarian processed my request. Since I never checked out books there before, I filled out a form. I naively asked her if she knew who

George Kaddish was and regretted my question as soon as it left my mouth. From first grade to high school, I was often asked if I knew who Bruce Lee was. Because I was the only Chinese in school, classmates reflexively assumed that I knew him or other remotely famous Asians. Now I was guilty of the same kind of faulty, naïve thinking. Thank goodness the librarian wasn't offended but she did look at me strangely yet sympathetically.

The next day, I opened up my books from the Jewish Community Center and learned that the Kaddish prayer was read aloud by mourners and praised God. Expecting words about sorrow or loss, I was surprised by its honorific and positive language. The Mourner's Kaddish prayer is not a lament but a resounding testimony of God's strength and power:

> Exalted and hallowed by God's greatness
> In this world of Your creation.
> May Your will be fulfilled
> And Your sovereignty revealed
> And the whole life of the whole house of Israel
> Speedily and soon. And say, Amen
> May You be blessed forever
> Even to all eternity.
> May You, most Holy One, be blessed,
> Praised and honored, extolled and glorified,
> Adored and exalted above all else.
> Blessed are You.
> Beyond all blessings and hymns, praises and consolations
> That may be uttered in this world,
> In the days of our lifetime,
> And say, Amen.
> May God, Who makes peace on high,
> Bring peace to all and to all Israel,
> And say, Amen. (3)

I read further and understood a little more from scholars and academics writing about the Kaddish prayer and Judaism. Although praising God is difficult when a loved one dies, it is customary to recite it because no single event in life tests a person's faith in God more than death, "The death of a loved one—especially an untimely death—confronts even the most faithful Jew with doubt." (4). By reciting it, the bereaved Jew is strengthening his faith in God despite personal loss.

While this was very interesting, I still didn't learn anything about George Kaddish. Discouraged, I took a break from my borrowed books from the Jewish Community Center and opened my other books for class. While reading, I noticed that 'YIVO' kept on popping up as a referenced source, 'YIVO Institute for Jewish Research, New York.' I'd noticed YIVO before my campus bookstore visit, as it was often referenced in the books listed in our syllabus. Since I was eager to find information, I decided that it couldn't hurt to ask this place about George Kaddish. Also, the word 'Institute' sounded big and established, and since it was in New York, I concluded that this place could possibly have more resources than Stanford University, the Jewish Community Center, and San Francisco State—all the libraries I'd already searched.

I asked my mother if I could make a long distance call to New York and mom said okay. A grown woman asking her mother to use the phone may seem odd but my mother had trust issues with phone companies, and I didn't want her to think that AT&T was bilking us. I dialed and waited for someone to answer. Several questions raced through my mind: Someone should know about George Kaddish. How many people took pictures of a dying neighbor who used his last remaining seconds on earth to write "Jews Revenge" in blood? How many people had this amount of courage during the Holocaust? Suddenly, a bright, kind voice answered, "Yes, I know who he is. He is not in New York, but lives in Hollywood, Florida." She had a very thick accent so I held onto every word. My heart started to beat faster and she asked, "Why do you want to know about him?" Calmly, I told her about the book mentioning George Kaddish and my quest to find out more about him since libraries didn't have much information. "You seem to be a very nice girl who wants to learn more. I don't have his number but he has a friend on the East Side, and his name is George Birman. He is also a Holocaust survivor. I will give you his number." (5).

My heart raced. I was going to tell my mother about the second long-distance phone call I was about to make but I was afraid of losing my nerve to call George Birman about George Kaddish's whereabouts. Sadistic acts, comparable to nothing the earth has ever known, were committed. Motherless children and childless mothers walked to their own deaths. What more did I need to know about the Holocaust? I recalled a black and white photo of the Babi Yar massacre where thirty thousand people died in two days; naked bodies were heaped one on top of the other in a massive pit. (6). Would I soon be talking to people who saw or photographed images worse than this? How much more did I need to know?

I didn't leave my desk, I stared at George Birman's phone number, and then a different fear emerged. Ignorance about Judaism and religion concerned me earlier and now I doubted my confidence. Introducing the Holocaust as a topic of conversation could be awkward and my current plan is cold-calling a man I didn't know about a man I didn't know much about. At the very least, I was going to remind survivors of a horrible event by just contacting them without warning and they may take offense at me, a perfect stranger, asking about painful experiences. Compounding my stress was this: George Birman could be someone who is a devout Jew and knows a lot about Judaism. Maybe I would ask disrespectful questions and not even know it. Childhood memories and my parents' voices resurfaced, "Don't ask questions." "Don't bother people." This had awkwardness written all over it. I knew nothing on top of nothing but I dialed and took a deep breath. My heart thumped louder. Luckily, my fears faded because George Birman was just like the lady at YIVO. He said I seemed like a nice girl. He was glad that students were studying the Holocaust and gave me George Kaddish's phone number. Furthermore, Birman asked me to call back anytime and to give George Kaddish his best. (7).

I carefully dialed George Kaddish's number in Hollywood, Florida. George's phone numbers loomed large on my notebook. "Hello?" an older voice chirped. "Sir, are you Mr. George Kaddish or Mr. Zvi Hirsch Kadushin?" "Yes, I am," he replied protectively and authoritatively. Nervously and enthusiastically, I said, "Mr. Kaddish you are alive!" Probably expecting to hear a telemarketer's pitch, he replied cantankerously, "Of course I am alive. I answered the phone! Who is this?" I apologized and tried to sound calm. I told him about George Birman of New York, the book at the Stanford bookstore, which published his photograph, and my fruitless searches in libraries for more information about him. This seemed to calm George and he asked if I had questions about the Holocaust or his experiences. Now was my chance and I carefully asked him about his name change from Zvi Hirsch Kadushin to George Kaddish. George's reply was immediate and bold, "I did it for the six million!" (8).

People thought George was crazy to change his name for the Jews murdered during the Holocaust. He said people described him as "meshuggeh." I later came to understand that "meshuggeh" means crazy. He quickly spoke about other topics related to the ghetto and Holocaust. He told me that the Nazis burned the ghetto to the ground and before that, they burned the ghetto's hospital with people inside of it. George spoke about the German shepherd dogs trained to lunge at the necks of Jews, countless round-ups of his friends and neighbors occurring at any given time or day, and the very, very cold winter of 1941. Although I was listening intently, the gravity of his voice, when he said "I did it for the six million!" was unforgettable. But instead of interrupting him, I planned to investigate further about his name change and how it related to the "six million" after our phone call.

In a stream-of-consciousness like style, George then talked about his methods of taking pictures in the ghetto. He spoke of his chronicling activities with pride and vigor. George built a camera especially designed to take pictures clandestinely. In some of his pictures, George positioned the lens just behind the buttonhole of his coat and activated the shutter with a subtle movement of his arm. He also took some pictures behind windows so that he wouldn't be seen and smuggled negatives and film in hospital crutches. George was ordered to work as an x-ray technician in a hospital for the Germans while they occupied Kovno. While he was carrying out his duties, George smuggled and traded supplies for film. As George was describing his experiences, I wanted to see him in person. Did his left or right hand activate the shutter? Did he hunch over? And if he did, did this affect the quality of his photos? While George was speaking, I didn't ask questions as his recollections seemed to wash over me like a great torrent. I did not want to disturb his flow of thoughts, interrupt him, and be disrespectful. Most importantly, I was mindful of his age and afraid that I was stressing him by asking him too many questions. Again, my plan: listen and record now, study and ask later.

Like George Birman, George Kaddish thought people lost interest in the Holocaust or did not believe it happened. Both were surprised that there were specific classes about the Holocaust. They knew there were books about the Holocaust but did not think a school or college would devote a semester or quarter's curriculum to it. More surprisingly, George Kaddish thought his photographs were forgotten. He seemed to slow down after saying this. I told him people did not forget and his photos were very important. At that moment, I vowed to myself that if I found any of his photos in books, I would photocopy the page, write him a letter, and send it to him. But most importantly though, I thought I was making George tired, so I thanked him for speaking with me. Incredibly George thanked me and said I could call anytime.

"The photographer, Zvi Kadushin (George Kadish) in Kovno, probably after the liberation." Date: After Aug 1944. Locale: Kovno. Photographer: George Kaddish. By courtesy of Beth Hatefutsoth, Photo Archive, Zvi Kadushin collection, Tel Aviv.

I leaned back in my chair. That day, three people and three phone calls affected me in a way I did not fully understand. I looked over my scrawled notes and quickly rewrote them before I forgot what each survivor said. I became the humble recipient of their every word. Possibly, each word for them was a spoken memory from a nightmare once lived. Maybe words and language itself were inadequate in describing the Holocaust. But today they accessed moments from a tragic and an unprecedented event to provide me with understanding. I felt indebted to them. Without warning, a faceless voice from three thousand miles away asked questions about experiences they probably wanted to forget.

That night I dreamed about figurative books filed in a section of a survivor's mind and heart. Was their book of Holocaust history a dusty volume intentionally shelved in a far away place with the hopes of forgetting? Or, was theirs a commonly checked-out book with a dog-eared cover and worn down spine? Did their book have the red, capitalized word 'DISCARD' harshly stamped onto the flesh of its pages? And when someone, like me, asks questions did they want to share their information or tell me that their "book" was lost, unavailable, or thrown away. The lady at YIVO, George Birman, and George Kaddish saw me at the 'check-out' desks in the libraries of their experiences. They generously opened up their books—their minds and hearts—gave me direction and encouraged me to learn more. I am incapable of giving them anything in return. Maybe the only thing I did was to show them that people did not forget.

I would call from time to time to check on George Kaddish. At the time I was taking two classes, one on modern European history and the other on Holocaust literature. I also worked at a congressman's office, first as an intern and later as a staff assistant. While studying and working, I ran across a couple of books with George's photography. I photocopied these pages and carefully highlighted George's name located in the tiny print at the sides or bottom of his published photographs. I wanted to show George that historians continued to educate the world through his photography. George needed to know that people did not forget the Holocaust or his courageous work. I told him that a letter was coming and he said he looked forward to receiving it. George also said he had photographs he wanted me to see at his house and invited me to come visit him in Hollywood, Florida. I was excited. I would finally see what we spoke so much about. Also, George wanted me to meet his daughter and I was really touched and honored. A few days later, I planned to tell George that I secured a plane ticket. That day came and I dialed George's number to tell him the good news. While it was ringing and I was waiting for George to answer, I thought about my first conversation with him. Back then, I was very tongue-tied and nervous but now I felt comfortable and had both a friend and teacher in George. My comfortable feelings however, turned to concern;

it usually didn't take George long to answer the phone. On the seventh ring or so, a different voice answered, "Hello?" the voice said. "Uh, yes ma'am, may I speak to Mr. George Kaddish if he is available? My name is Catherine Gong." After what seemed to be an eternity, the voice said, "My father died four days ago. I am his daughter."

I tried to quickly process information from the words the voice uttered. To reassure George's daughter that a total stranger wasn't on the phone, I told her my name again, how sorry I was, and that he was a kind and brave man who taught me about what he did during the Holocaust. She thanked me for my condolences and said her name was Georgia. It moved me to hear George in her name. By George's choice, his last name, "Kaddish," is identified with those lost to Nazi destruction ("I did it for the six million!"); by intention as well, George's first name is linked to his daughter, Georgia—the namesake of his wife's creation. Often, I've heard the phrase, "What's in a name?" and it usually prompts a reply implying inadequacy but not in this case. I did not fully understand what all this meant, as I was shocked, sad, and just learning that George died but Georgia—his daughter's name—was George's way of linking his identity with not only loss and annihilation but with hope and regeneration.

I told Georgia about the conversations I had with her father. I told her about how his photography taught me the importance of human rights. Georgia listened intently and added that she did not know what to do with her father's photo collection. I asked her if George's photos were in a fire-proof safe. She said they weren't. In an earlier conversation, George told me he was going to leave the last portion of his photo collection to his daughter. Again, Georgia asked me if I had any suggestions about how we could preserve his legacy.

After the war, George amassed a large photo collection and divided it into three parts. In an earlier conversation, George told me he had distributed two portions of his photo collection to two museums: a museum in Israel (Beth Hatefutsoth) and the other in Washington, D.C. (United States Holocaust Memorial Museum). The last portion, as he told me in what was one of the last conversations we shared together, was with him at home in Hollywood, Florida. Furthermore, George said he divided his collection between these two locations precisely because he wanted it widely distributed so that people from all over could see his photos and learn about the Kovno ghetto. Because of these conversations with George, I told Georgia about the one person I knew at the Simon Wiesenthal Center and Museum of Tolerance in Los Angeles, California. I didn't know much about the establishment at the time but its mission of preserving Holocaust history and eliminating intolerance was well known. Should this west coast museum become the location of George's last batch of photography, his images would be spread evenly on two coasts in America. In order to think about this more carefully, I told Georgia that I'd call her back in thirty minutes. I closed my bedroom door and sat quietly. It seemed as if a precious, orphaned baby was left at my doorstep and now it was my duty to find a guardian who'd be forever concerned and mindful of its safety.

I phoned Georgia back and she was kind and thanked me for returning her call. Again, she asked me about what should she do about her father's photographs. I told her my thoughts about the Los Angeles museum. Indeed, Georgia wanted me to introduce her to my acquaintance, a rabbi, at the Simon Wiesenthal Museum of Tolerance to find out if he was interested in obtaining George's collection for preservation. After promising Georgia that I would initiate her introduction to the museum and the rabbi, Georgia then asked me to write her father's obituary. I was honored but felt incapable. However I wanted to do anything I could to reduce the burden of a mourning daughter so I agreed to do it. Before our conversation ended, I told her I would keep her updated and keep my promises.

I slumped in my chair. That day, one person and one phone call affected me in a way I am still trying to understand. Numbly, I phoned the rabbi I knew at the Los Angeles museum. The rabbi told me that I did a "mitzvah" and that meant I did a good deed. I started on George's obituary. I'd never written one before. I would try to put the essence of all the conversations George and I shared in every word. The paper felt odd and pencil seemed heavy. My pencil seemed imbalanced, clumsy, and weighed down with an incomparable burden; its lead was brittle and sharp and each stroke wounded the smoothness of the paper it was scraping up against. The conversations George and I had were sometimes heartbreaking and it occurred to me that I had knowledge about his recording activities but what I didn't know was why he named himself after the Jewish death prayer. I only knew George's resolute response, "I did it for the six million!" I never got to ask George. I felt regretful and incapable but I did the best I could with George's obituary and as promised, I faxed it to the Jewish Telegraphic Agency:

> George Kaddish (Zvi Hirsch Kadushin) of Hollywood, Florida was a Holocaust survivor. During the Holocaust, Mr. Kaddish risked his life to bear witness and photographed daily life in the Kovno Ghetto of Lithuania. Mr. Kaddish is survived by his daughter, Georgia Geary, from Montana.

I fulfilled George's mission and Georgia's promise; George's photos would be evenly distributed and I wrote his obituary for his daughter but there seemed to be more to do.

I didn't leave the house and just stayed in my bedroom for a long time. My mother pushed the acceptance letters from colleges I'd applied to under my door. I was planning to get my second master's degree and looked forward to studying more about the Holocaust. I should have been happy about my college acceptances but I didn't move much and when I did, it was hard to breathe.

Something inside me tore. I was not even interested about the Kaddish prayer anymore and how it could be linked to George's last name. I returned my books back to the Jewish Community Center. I quit going to class and when I went back, I hardly spoke to anyone. I felt I had lost a favorite teacher. The rabbi from the Simon Wiesenthal Center and Museum of Tolerance called me and reassured me that George's collection was indeed safe and that his representative met with Georgia in Florida and purchased the last portion of George's photography. (9).

But I needed to do more. Again, I thought about the questions I should have asked George. I felt frozen but then something happened. I brushed off my bed covers and brushed my teeth and hair. I went downstairs and told my mother that I did open the acceptance letters she'd set aside for me but I told her I didn't want to go to graduate school. I wanted to go to Los Angeles and see George's photographs.

His Body of Work

It was clear. I didn't want to go to graduate school. I wondered what my mother's response would be. What would my father or brother say? I told them I wanted to see George's photos. I didn't learn much about George while I read about the Kaddish prayer in my borrowed library books but maybe seeing George's photos would give me more insight about George Kaddish as a person and his last name. My family asked questions. No, I didn't know how large George's photo collection was. And no, I didn't know exactly what George photographed, as the only photos I'd seen were the ones in the book I purchased from the campus bookstore and the others I'd photocopied and sent to George before he died. Why should I go to the east coast and attend graduate school when I could stay on the west coast and look at what George risked his life for? Maybe what George chronicled will tell me something about what he valued? I think my father wondered if I was just postponing graduate school. A few of the colleges I applied to such as Columbia University and Brandeis deferred acceptances. As I told them, if I returned from Los Angeles unhappy, I would then head eastward to study. I told them it would really only cost me a twelve-hour drive to and from Los Angeles and two tanks of gas. In my life, I was either working or studying or both, and my current proposal didn't fit in either category. They looked at me sympathetically. I felt as if I was at the Jewish Community Center's library again and uttered more unwise and uninformed thoughts but surprisingly, they offered me their resources and blessing.

I phoned the rabbi at the Simon Wiesenthal Center and Museum of Tolerance and asked if I could come and look at George's photo collection. He agreed and said George's photo collection needed attention. I packed up my best clothes, reassured my family I would be back, filled up my gas tank, and bought a map. As I drove southward down the long ribbon of highway snaking through Southern California's low hills, I thought about George's photographs. Maybe what George photographed will tell me something about why he risked his life and changed his name.

Since I left San Francisco early in the morning, I arrived at the museum at around 10.00 a.m. The rabbi expected me at 12.00 p.m., so I went to a nearby gas station, used the restroom to re-brush my hair, and thought about possible answers to questions he might ask. I was fully aware of my lack of knowledge of many things but gathered up as much information as I could in the hopes I could complete a full sentence and not stammer when spoken to. Upon arrival, the rabbi thanked me again for informing him about George's photo collection and for the obituary I'd written for his daughter, Georgia; and he even wrote me a kind letter of appreciation as well, which doubled as a letter of recommendation to colleges if I had to reapply again.

בס״ד

To whom it may concern:

This is to introduce Catherine Gong, who has worked closely with the Simon Wiesenthal Center and Museum of Tolerance during the last 2 years on a voluntary basis on numerous projects.

Most recently, Catherine helped curate the acclaimed "Visas For Life" exhibition at our museum. She was also instrumental helping the Center to acquire the George Kaddish collection, an extremely important photo collection taken by the late photographer in the Kovno Ghetto.

I highly recommend Ms. Gong to your graduate program. Her participation in serious Holocaust studies will certainly enhance and deepen her well-established commitment to promoting Holocaust remembrance throughout the community.

Sincerely,

Rabbi Abraham Cooper
Associate Dean

The rabbi introduced me to the museum's photo archivist and said I'd assist her in organizing George's photography. I pledged to do my best for George and maybe in the process, I would finally have an opportunity to know more about him, his work, and why he changed his name from Kadushin to Kaddish.

I went downstairs as the rabbi directed and met the archivist. She pointed me to a corner where there were at least six or seven stacked rectangular boxes having an approximate base of four feet and height of three. Each box had a thickness of about four inches. I was standing near a hallowed source. I didn't dare touch anything but my eyes continued to measure and witness. Velvety layers of dust and silken cobwebs coated George's boxes and they formed protective seams covering the small tears and rips in the corrugated lids. There were places indicating recent contact though, as the dust patterns were interrupted by darker, cleaner blotches in the shapes of fingers and a hand's heel; these recent prints probably belonged to Georgia, the rabbi, or the Museum's representative. But this didn't matter because I knew for sure, even without lifting one lid, that George's fingerprints were not only in these boxes but his heart and soul. George's photo collection traveled all the way from Kovno to Hollywood, Florida and now to Los Angeles, California. I imagined George's boxes in the cargo space of a plane and the potentially bumpy ride it took. Or maybe it came by a freight train or truck? But it didn't matter, these boxes at one time were thousands of miles away from me and now they were only inches from my hands.

Once I'd heard someone say, "A journey of a thousand miles begins where you are standing." This Obi Wan Kenobi-esqe phrase seemed to be spoken from someone who came from my family's homeland—a country where scholars wore silk, brocade robes and lived in monasteries. This proverb provoked magical feelings inside me and it seemed that this stack of boxes would become a time machine and transport me to a different time and place in Europe.

The archivist gave me special cotton gloves, glassines to put the photos in, a measuring tape, a special number two pencil, and a magnifying glass. She instructed me to dust George's photos and insert them into plastic protective covers. Afterwards, I'd determine a photo's dimensions. Little did I know that the simple acts of dusting and measuring photographs would indeed pull me back to another era.

Faces and Names

As I was removing cobwebs from George's photos one by one, I started recognizing names that seemed strangely familiar. On the backs of some photos, George wrote the names of people he photographed. He also recorded the locations of some of his photos too. The other names of people and places from George's photos came from information sheets accompanying some of his images. At the top of these documents were the letters "USHMM" bolded and centered. As I soon learned, USHMM stands for the United States Holocaust Memorial Museum. Since George's donation to this museum in D.C., the USHMM archived his collection and organized the photography for Holocaust survivors and the public. Over time, visitors to the USHMM identified the locations and people in many of George's photographs and it was this information that was now shared with the Simon Wiesenthal Museum of Tolerance. While looking at these information sheets and George's images, I imagined what it was like to find someone you knew staring back at you from a time of great suffering. And if you shared the same last name as the photographed person, could you see yourself there and know you were only saved and did not have to endure because you were born in a different time or place. Or, as a child or descendant of a survivor, what is it like to see your parents or grandmother in a photograph and know they faced certain death and witnessed it? Unimaginable questions from an unimaginable time. Bravery from these friends, relatives, and spouses helped the United States Holocaust Memorial Museum and now the Los Angeles museum fill in the blanks and it was their information that was printed before me now. Combined with George Kaddish's hand-written inscriptions, each word on every USHMM document was speaking to me and its voice bore witness and revealed to me, without reservation, personal loss.

I came across a photograph thickly covered in dust and grime. With the archival brush, I carefully dusted the light debris off. I started from the corners and worked my way to the center. It was a photograph of performing musicians. Right in the middle of the photo was a woman. Her face was almost a blur but she was clearly in the background. According to the USHMM document, her name was Maya Gladstein. The two men in the forefront of the photograph, one conducting the small orchestra and the other a violinist, were on the right and left of Gladstein; the positions of the conductor's baton and the violinist's bow framed her face in a moment captured in time. I read the USHMM information sheet further and learned that Gladstein was a violinist and performed in the ghetto orchestra. I read that clandestine performances were held in the Kovno ghetto because the Nazis outlawed music and ordered the destruction of all musical instruments. Furthermore, there was a scheduled "Intellectuals Action," in which Jewish authors, academics, and the musicians of Kovno were rounded up and shot. (10). All of this information was sobering and difficult to grasp but what loomed larger was her name, 'Maya Gladstein.' Her name sounded very familiar. I just did not know how or where I heard about her before.

I set Maya Gladstein aside and started on another pile. After several hours of dusting and covering George's pictures, I took a walk. Maya Gladstein. Her name sounded very familiar and I still didn't know why but then something extraordinary happened. It seemed I was witnessing some kind of dialogue occurring between the USHMM document and George's image. Then another voice contributed to this conversation.

I found out why I recalled her name. I'd read about Maya Gladstein before in a memoir documenting a teenager's experiences during the Holocaust. About a year earlier, a local historian in San Francisco introduced me to a Holocaust survivor. His name was Solly Ganor. At the time I was an intern at a non-profit organization and its mission was to record testimonies from Holocaust survivors and concentration camp liberators. This local historian often contributed his efforts to this organization and one day he visited the office with his colleague, Solly. In my first meeting with Solly, he told me about his published diary, *Light One Candle*. I immediately bought and read it and it is in this published diary that Solly mentions a woman named Maya Gladstein. Naturally, I did not commit the full contents of Solly's book to memory but I wondered if there were more familiar sounding names in Solly's book and George's photos. The hopes of matching more names in *Light One Candle* with more faces in George's collection quickened my steps back to the archives. Upon my return, the closet storing George's boxes of photography was not just hallowed ground anymore but the entire room seemed to transform into an almost holy, reverent sanctum. One may only see a tiny room underneath a staircase with a broom in the corner and one bare light bulb but for me this room was the location where history came alive.

On this day, my first day, several hours felt like a few minutes. I didn't have *Light One Candle* in Los Angeles. I called my mother and asked her if

I could come home right away. I told her about what I thought was happening in the archives room. I filled up my gas tank and began to drive. While I was driving I wondered out loud and drove faster. Could George's photos really match the people in Solly's book? Before reading *Light One Candle*, I didn't know anything about Lithuania and after I read Solly's book, I read other books written by Holocaust survivors from Poland but not Lithuania. With the exception of George's photographs at the archives, I hadn't studied or read anything about Lithuania since Solly's memoir or the book, *The World Must Know*, containing that small caption about George's activities during the Holocaust. What were the chances of Solly and George being at the same place and time during the Holocaust? I was anxious to get home and finally got there. My mother welcomed me home and I spent the day with her and phoned my brother and father. The next day, I grabbed *Light One Candle* and any other books about the Holocaust from my footlocker. If I was wrong about *Light One Candle*, I could also re-read the other books as well. I needed to find Maya Gladstein in one of these books. She just *had* to be there. I drove back to Los Angeles. Next day, I went back to the archives room with *Light One Candle* and a stack of post-it notes.

Re-reading and hunting for names paid off; I found Solly's paragraph about musicians who secretly held concerts in the Kovno ghetto. According to Solly's book, Maya Gladstein was a Lithuanian violinist who played in the ghetto orchestra. I read further and found other people that Solly mentioned and George photographed. Their names were Michael Hofmekler, Alexander Stupfel, and two other musicians known simply as the Bornstein brothers. In the following paragraph from *Light One Candle*, Solly explains that his father assisted the musicians with equipment and supplies,

> Since father was in charge of supplying the orchestra, I became acquainted with most of the members. The conductor was the well-known musician Michael (Misha) Hofmekler, friend of Father's . . . Then there was Alexander (Abrasha) Stupfel, first violinist . . . the Bornstein brothers [and]Maya Gladstein . . . and many others . . . (11)

Hofmekler, Stupfel, and Bornstein; indeed, there were other written names matching George's photographed faces.

In the following pages, George's photographs and text from the United States Holocaust Memorial Museum and Solly Ganor's *Light One Candle* are featured. Survivor testimonies from the USHMM and Solly Ganor's *Light One Candle* are in bold text unless otherwise noted. Also, my observations are in normal type unless otherwise noted.

"**Pictured are Alexander (Shaya) Stupel, playing the violin and Michael Leo Hofmekler, conducting. Maya Gladshtein is seated behind in the center.**" **Date: 1944. Locale: Kovno Ghetto. Photographer: George Kadish/Zvi Kadushin. Photo Credit: USHMM, courtesy of Robert W. Hofmekler.**

Despite the Nazis attempt to strip Jews of their cultural identity, Kovno's Jews held concerts.

"**Jewish police gathering at the main gate to the ghetto. Standing first on the left is Avrasha Stupel, who played the violin with the Kovno Ghetto orchestra.**" **Date: 1941-1943. Locale: Kovno Ghetto. Photographer: George Kadish/Zvi Kadushin. Photo Credit: USHMM, Courtesy of George Kadish/Zvi Kadushin.**

I learned further from the USHMM archives that Avrasha also had a brother named Boris.

Avrasha Stupel's brother, "... **Boris Stupel, standing guard at the entrance to the offices of the Jewish Council. A sign posted on the wall indicates hours of operation.**" (12).

Like his brother, Avrasha, Boris Stupel, "... **was a famous violinist before the war ...**" But Boris also became a police officer in the ghetto in an accidental way. On August 18, 1941, the Nazis "... killed 534 of the ghetto's most highly educated men ..." (13). Because of this massacre, which was later known as the 'Intellectuals Action,' most musicians feared to declare their professions and credentials. "In order to provide them with a 'useful' occupation, the Jewish Council made all of them policemen." (14).

"The Kovno ghetto Jewish police force was created on order of the German occupation authorities in July 1941, even before ..." all the Jews were removed from their homes and into the ghetto. (15). The function of the police force "was to maintain order and discipline in the ghetto and to enforce the orders of the Jewish Council ... the police maintained high moral standards and gradually gained the respect of the population. On November 11, 1942, every member of the police force signed an oath pledging to act for the welfare of the Jewish community ..." (16).

Throughout the ghetto's existence, Boris Stupel played in the ghetto orchestra.

Date: 1941-1944. Locale: Kovno Ghetto. Photographer: George Kadish/Zvi Kadushin. By courtesy of Beth Hatefutsoth, Photo Archive, Zvi Kadushin collection, Tel Aviv.

"Boris Stupel . . . carries his violin in the ghetto." Date: August 1942- March 1944. Locale: Kovno Ghetto. Photographer: George Kadish/Zvi Kadushin. Published Source: USHMM archives and USHMM *Hidden History of the Kovno Ghetto*.

Even though I initially learned about Avrasha Stupel from Solly's book, the USHMM's archives notes informed me further about Avrasha's brother, Boris. Gathering testimonies from different survivors became valuable in learning more about Kovno's cultural life.

Pictured at right Yitzhak Bornstein.—"The orchestra consisted of 35 instrumentalists and five vocalists led by the noted conductor Michael Leo Hofmekler and the concert master Stupel. Performances were held bi-weekly, and a total of 80 concerts were given during the ghetto's history . . . many in the ghetto felt it was unseemly to hold concerts in a place of mourning . . . However, despite these criticisms, most felt that the concerts . . . rais[ed] the level of morale in the ghetto." Date: Circa 1943. Locale: Kovno Ghetto. Photographer: George Kadish/Zvi Kadushin. Photo Credit: USHMM, courtesy of George Kadish/Zvi Kadushin.

In *Light One Candle*, Solly recalls, "I thought I would never hear music again. The orchestra was playing Tchaikovsky. It was the *1812 Overture*, and as the music swelled up from the pit [,] I couldn't hold back my tears." (17).

I re-read the entire book to resuscitate my memory. Solly's words about Tchaikovsky were especially moving. Jews attempted to express beauty and culture despite the terror surrounding them. In the following lines from Solly's *Light One Candle*, a young Solly praises a man named Chaim, who teaches him and his best friend, Cooky Kopelman, the value of music,

> While the music played, Chaim would sit in his old rocking
> chair with his eyes closed and [with the] expression of bliss on
> his face . . . Cooky [was] also enthralled . . . Music is the most
> enriching and rewarding of all the human arts. Chaim helped me
> appreciate music much more than I had before . . . Cooky was
> fascinated by the old man. To him, Chaim was the epitome of
> wisdom, a master of the arts.(18).

Playing music was punishable by death and so was the very act of taking pictures of a concert or for that matter, taking pictures of any kind. Despite the danger, George's images of this clandestine performance as well as his other images of the Kovno ghetto were kept safe with the help of Yehuda Zupowitz. According to the USHMM archives, Zupowitz was a member of the ghetto's police force and very active in the resistance movement. Furthermore, George entrusted Zupowitz with hiding his photography. When I first came to the Simon Wiesenthal's archives, I thought of only George's guardianship protecting Kovno's time capsule but now I thought of Yehuda Zupowitz and his careful, conscientious hands. Sadly, Zupowitz was murdered, along with others who participated in the ghetto's underground activities. According to Solly Ganor's *Light One Candle*, Zupowitz was tortured and burned alive on a pyre of corpses. A fellow police officer, who was also beaten badly, reveals to Solly what happened to George's brave comrade:

> . . . [Yehuda] Zupowitz [was] also brought before us and tortured
> horribly. [He] refused to speak, and met the same fate, . . . along
> with the others who knew secrets and refused to divulge them.
> They died in agony. All [of] their bodies were thrown on top of a
> tall stack of corpses, and burned in the same pyre.(19).

To protect George's chronicle of Kovno's life, Zupowitz sacrificed his own. I looked at the round metal containers of film and negatives stacked quietly on the shelf. I imagined Zupowitz tucking these containers under his coat and moving stealthily in the ghetto; Zupowitz passes the ghetto's guardsmen and outside its gates with George's film. After looking over his shoulder, Zupowitz kneels to the ground, and with several swift movements, he cups his hands, uses his fingers as a shovel, and eases George's time capsule deeply into the earth. My imagined bird's eye view sees Zupowitz's faithful hands and fingers and the brown soil sprinkling the tops of George's film containers.

"Deputy Police Chief Yehuda Zupowitz at his desk in the Kovno Ghetto." Date: 1944. Locale: Kovno Ghetto. Photographer: George Kadish/Zvi Kadushin. Photo Credit: USHMM, courtesy of Yehudit Katz Sperling.

On my first day at the museum's archives room, my hands gripped two metal containers that were flat, round, and heavy. Shaped like two small-sized pizzas, these containers stored George's film. When I opened their rusty round covers, there were yards and yards of brownish-black celluloid tightly coiled inside. An undefinable yet undeniable sensation surged through my fingers, as Kovno's chronicle of life and death was in my hands. When I learned that Yehuda Zupowitz helped George obtain film and hide Kovno's time capsule, I thought about the courage he summoned to bear witness. According to the *Hidden History of the Kovno Ghetto*, **"Kadish recognized early on the danger of losing his precious collection. He enlisted the assistance of Yehuda Zupowitz, a high-ranking officer in the ghetto's Jewish police, to help hide negatives and prints."** (20).

After I learned more about Yehuda Zupowitz's brave deeds, I decided to write Solly Ganor, the author of the published diary, *Light One Candle*. I told Solly about the pictures I was matching with his book and I wanted to know more about Zupowitz. I was lucky. Solly responded.

In a letter to me, Solly Ganor wrote about Zupowitz's bravery; I'd never received a letter from Israel before and it came to my mother's house, **"Yudel indeed helped Kadushin to hide the negatives. He got him the contact with the Lithuanians to obtain the films . . . some of the negatives were actually sent for safe keeping with Lithuanians outside the ghetto and after the war, Kadushin got them back."** (21).

Zupowitz was later shot and his body thrown on a pyre of corpses for his underground activities, **"Zupowitz never revealed his knowledge of Kadish's work or the location of his collection, even during the 'Police Action' of March 27, 1944, when Zupowitz was tortured and killed at the Fort IX prison."** (22).

"Deputy Police Chief Yehuda Zupowitz poses with his wife, Dita, in their apartment . . ." Date: March 1944. Locale: Kovno Ghetto. Photographer: George Kadish/Zvi Kadushin. Photo Credit: USHMM, courtesy of Yehudit Katz Sperling.

Solly further wrote about the research notes and facsimiles of George's photos I'd sent him. Solly's correspondence helped me immensely during this time, **"[about] the photocopies you have sent," "with . . . Zupowitz, and the unidentified woman on it, I am glad to tell you that the unidentified**

woman is his wife, Jehudit Katz-Zupowitz . . . She is the sister of a good friend of mine, Zwi Katz." (23).

Two weeks after George took this picture of Zupowitz and his wife in their ghetto apartment, he was arrested during the Police Action on March 27, 1944. On this date, the Nazis, **"seeking information about the ghetto's underground and hiding places, ordered 140 members of the Jewish police to assemble."** (24). Many, like Yehuda Zupowitz were immediately arrested, tortured, and killed.

Without Zupowitz, George's photographs would not have survived. Without him, I would have never had the opportunity to see George's photographs next to Solly's words. Having both the photographs and diary side by side deepened the sympathy I had for people like George, Maya Gladstein, Solly, and Michael Hofmeckler. For instance, on my desk is George's photo of Hofmeckler and his face is only inches away from Solly's words written about him. This may seem uneventful and ordinary to many but for me it wasn't. At that moment, I confirmed that all knew each other's families and friends and witnessed each other's struggles. And in this rare case, all enjoyed a small piece of happiness in the ghetto. Looking at George's concert photographs, while reading about Solly's love of music and this sense of community brought me closer to a kind of witnessing.

I had a dream that night. I ate a good meal, nested in my bedcovers, saw the insides of my eyelids, and fell asleep. *A partially unrolled spool of film is on fire. Orange-yellow flames licking the notched edges of a filmstrip melt and distort smiling faces and stitched yellow stars. Celluloid is cracking, popping and burning my skin. And flames in the shape of thin, flickering arrowheads pierce and liquefy the film's perfect rectangles once framing a town and its children.*

I mean no disrespect to those who have survived the ghettos, camps, or death marches and assume I have 'witnessed' as they did; disrespecting survivors is my worst fear and is not my intention. However, the sources of information I grouped together on my desk brought me closer to "witnessing" a rare dialogue; I could see exactly what I was reading about. During my experiences of reading Solly's words and seeing George's photographs, I felt a sense of elevated pain and fear. In a book, text is often accompanied by photography chronicling an approximate time. In a documentary, sometimes an image generally captures what occurred. But in this case, the front and backs of George's photos "dialogued" with Solly's text about the same moments and places, and were about the same people and their lives. This kind of "real-time witnessing," an experience I never knew before, was the result of linking two primary sources of information from two Holocaust survivors who escaped death from a location where more than 95% of Kovno's Jews died. (25). On an emotional level, linking Solly's literary equivalent to George's visual testimony brought me closer to a kind of re-enactment. It was more than a picture or a book 'coming to life.' Rather, the juxtaposition of both bodies of work helped me "witness" Solly Ganor, George Kaddish, Maya Gladstein, and Michael Hofmeckler's love and sense of urgency for music during a time of great sorrow.

This kind of "dialogue" however took an emotional toll on me. When the images in George's photographs and words in Solly's text became increasingly dire, "witnessing" feels sobering. The turning of a page or dusting of a photo can lead to discovery but what remains is a lasting feeling of grim pensiveness. Looking at George's photos together while re-reading Solly Ganor's book was unlike anything I've seen or read since. I still don't have the words.

In the next few weeks I found a few more of George's photos containing people Solly knew in *Light One Candle*: Yankale Bergman, Moshe Levin, Elkahnan Elkes, and Beno Lipzer, the man who saved the life of Solly's sister. While confirming my findings, Solly even saw himself in one of George's photographs.

"Jews buying and selling . . . in the Kovno Ghetto." Date: 1941-1943. Locale: Kovno Ghetto. Photographer: George Kadish/Zvi Kadushin. Published Source: *The Hidden History of the Kovno Ghetto*, United States Holocaust Memorial Museum.

Pictured is the young Solly Ganor carrying a basket. When Solly met up with me in the archives room at the Simon Wiesenthal Center and Museum of

Tolerance, Solly identified himself in George's photograph, while confirming my other findings. This was the highlight during my months of research. In his diary, *Light One Candle*, Solly discusses making extra money for his family by selling his mother's bread on Kovno's streets, **"Mother baked buns . . . . And I sold them on Varniu Street so we could buy other necessities. I became a small entrepreneur . . ."** (26).

"Group portrait of children who served as runners for Kovno ghetto organizations. Among those pictured is Yankele Bergman (front row, right side). While working for the Jewish Council, he helped hide the ghetto's secret archive." Date: 1941-1943. Locale: Kovno Ghetto. Photographer: George Kadish/Zvi Kadushin. Photo Credit: USHMM, courtesy of Yad Vashem Archives.

When Solly looked at the photographs I'd spread out on the long conference tables at the Simon Wiesenthal Center and Museum of Tolerance, my face brightened when he pointed to Yankele Bergman, a runner or a messenger who served the Jewish Council and ghetto's resistance movement. Solly noted that Bergman lived in Israel. Very few of George's subjects survived, thus Solly's confirmation of Bergman's survival helped me get through the rest of my research. After looking at all of the images of George's that I'd displayed, Solly wanted to follow up with Bergman, **"Now I will try to track [him] down. I know that he is in Israel . . . as soon as I will hear from him, I will let you know."** (27).

**"Dr. Elkhanan Elkes, head of the Jewish Council of the Kovno ghetto."
Date: 1941. Locale: Kovno Ghetto. Photographer: George Kadish/Zvi
Kadushin. Photo Credit: USHMM, courtesy of Yad Vashem Photo
Archives.**

**"Dr. Elkhanan Elkes (1879-1944) was a Jewish physician who, during
the German occupation of Lithuania, assumed the leadership of the
Jewish community in the Kovno ghetto."** (28).

Throughout the Holocaust, Jewish Council Leader Elkes constantly attempted to
reason with German authorities. When the Nazis demanded a certain number of
Jews to assemble for deportation, Elkes did his best to reduce quotas explaining
that Germans needed more Jews for Kovno's ghetto workforce or the Luftwaffe's
proposed airfield, etc. Despite Elkes' efforts, the Germans oftentimes would
threaten and carry out reprisals taking even more lives.

The pressures of Elkes' position were also appreciated by Solly. In his diary,
Solly writes, **"Dr. Elchanan Elkes, a man father respected headed the
'Der Yiddisher Kommitet'—The Jewish Committee."** (29). **"Dr. Elkes
and the Jewish Council continued to negotiate with the German military
and civil authorities to keep the ghetto intact, arranging fresh bribes
whenever new German officials and guards replaced the old, winning a
few reprieves and clemencies for the inmates. Murders continued . . . ,
but at a slower pace."** (30).

"Three Jewish policemen patrol a street of the Kovno ghetto. Left to right: Moshe Levin, chief of the Jewish police and a member of the underground, and his two deputies: Yehuda Zupowitz and Tanchum Aronstamm." Date: 1941-1944. Locale: Kovno Ghetto. Photographer: George Kadish/Zvi Kadushin. By courtesy of Beth Hatefutsoth, Photo Archive, Zvi Kadushin collection, Tel Aviv.

Like Deputy Zupowitz, Captain Moshe Levin participated in the ghetto's resistance activities. Levin was ruthlessly tortured during interrogation and died without revealing George's photographic chronicle and the ghetto's underground plans against the Nazis and pro-Nazi Lithuanians. Levin was known for his rigid but effective leadership.

In *Light One Candle,* Solly learns about Captain Levin's fate from a ghetto police officer who narrowly escaped death from the Germans, **"Moshe Levin . . . had been very active in the underground, and helped many young men to escape to the partisans' groups. The Gestapo and the SS had their informants . . . and decided to get rid of Moshe Levin and his police force."** **'Our chief . . . [was]'** **'. . . beaten so mercilessly that we barely recognized [him].'** **'But we recognized Moshe's voice.'** **Levin said, "Listen they are trying to extract information from us about the hiding places and** the resistance movement in the Ghetto. Comrades, let us die with dignity! Not a word to the murderers!" "Moshe Levin was a very strict boss, even a bastard sometimes, but when he spoke to us that day, I knew that I was standing before a hero." "SS Obersturmbahnfuehrer Kitel . . . was known for his sadism . . ." [but] "no amount of torture brought a single word from him." "Then Kitel leaned too near, and Moshe spat a mouthful of blood and saliva into his face. The infuriated Kitel couldn't control himself. Drawing his revolver he shot Moshe dead." Like Yehuda Zupowitz, Moshe Levin's body was thrown on a stack of corpses "almost two meters high" and burned. "Kitel knew that they knew, yet they did not speak." (31).

"Beno Lipzer at the main gate of the Kovno ghetto. Lipzer served as a liaison between the Gestapo and the ghetto." Date: August 1943. Locale: Kovno Ghetto. Photographer: George Kadish/Zvi Kadushin. Photo Credit: USHMM, courtesy of Yad Vashem Archives.

Whereas Elkes' position was perceived as untenable because he constantly had to negotiate Jewish lives with the Gestapo, Lipzer seemed to savor his position as a 'savior' of the ghetto's Jews. Even though Lipzer was seen as less than altruistic, he nonetheless saved Solly's sister, Fanny from certain death. As Solly recalls in *Light One Candle*, "[she was] caught buying flour with a Lithuanian, and unfortunately, the Lithuanian was stealing it from the German army supply depot. Usually any Jew who fell into the hands of the Gestapo for even the

smallest infraction was sent to . . . execution. Fanny's crime, trading in goods stolen from the German army, was of the severest kind. There was no hope for her at all." Solly's mother, as a last resort to save her daughter, suggested a meeting with Beno Lipzer, **'. . . let us do our damndest to save her, ... Let's go to Lipzer.' Lipzer "was in charge of the brigade that worked for the Gestapo in Kaunas (Kovno) and in contact with high Gestapo officials . . . In this position Lipzer frequently managed to free various Jews who fell into the hands of the Gestapo. Lipzer earned the gratitude of many families by saving their loved ones from certain death. To them [he] was the all-powerful defender of the downtrodden . . ." "Lipzer, who fancied himself a protector of the common man, would intervene on their behalf . . ."** (32).

Solly's family also had another advantage. Before the war, Lipzer was beaten up by thugs and Solly's brother saved and rescued him. Lipzer swore that he would always remember. In *Light One Candle*, Solly's mother flatly stated, **"It is time to collect the debt."** (33).

In the end, Solly's family had to provide money, gold, or other valuables to Lipzer. In turn, Lipzer bribed the German officials and successfully negotiated Fanny's return, **"From a distance, we saw Fanny's familiar figure. She was limping, and as she came nearer we could see her face was swollen and discolored. But she walked through the gate with her head held high. I guess she wanted us to see that the Germans didn't break her spirit. Then we grabbed her and were hugging and crying together."** (34).

Solly Ganor's book, *Light One Candle* was not the only book that helped me learn about the people in the Kovno ghetto. Before George died, I'd only read Solly's memoir chronicling the Kovno ghetto when the Germans occupied Lithuania. But while I was archiving George's collection, my knowledge about this region grew as the archives' library had books written by other Lithuanian survivors: *Heroism and Bravery in Lithuania: 1941-1945* by Alex Faitelson, *The Hidden History of the Kovno Ghetto* by The United States Holocaust Memorial Museum (USHMM), *Kaddish for Kovno* by William W. Mishell and *Responsa from the Holocaust* by Rabbi Oshry. All of these books helped me understand George and Solly's experiences better.

Several memorable highlights in this period of dusting, measuring, researching, and matching also occurred. One was when Solly came to the archives room. So that Solly could read his own words describing the people and places he knew and see George's pictures chronicling these same people and places, I retyped Solly's whole book and glued photocopies of George's pictures to these typed pages. Solly thanked me for matching George's pictures to his book even when I would send images that were horrific, "Thanks for the letters and the additional Kadushin photocopies. You have done a great job in matching passages from my book . . . Concerning the grisly photos, please do send them. They are important evidence of what the Nazis did to us." (35).

Herzelia, November 15, 1998

Dear Catherine,

Thanks for the letters and the additional Kadushin photo copies. You have done a great job in matching passages from my book. Your book idea is good and I am all for it.

We will have to get permission from my publisher, Kodansha America Inc., and from the Simon Wiesenthal Center, but I am sure that won't pose a problem, or at least I don't think it will. I will do my best to get their consent, but have you considered who would publish the book? Perhaps I could approach Kodansha with the idea.

Anyway, I too have been working on it and have sent some passages matching the photos to Eric Saul sometimes ago. Perhaps we can combine the two and pick which one would be more suitable.

However, before such a book can be published we will have to wait after the exhibition that Eric Saul is putting up at the Simon Wiesenthal C enter in July next year. Or, on the second thought perhaps it can come out at the same time and be presented at the opening of the exhibition. We will have to decide about it.

Two of the photo copies you have sent us with Judel Zupowitz and the unidentified woman on it, I am glad to tell you that the unidentified woman is his wife, Jehudit Katz-Zupowitz. I spoke to her yesterday. She is the sister of a good friend of mine Zwi Katz. Photos # 112 & 113.

She told me the following:

Yudel indeed helped Kadushin to hide the negatives. He got him the contact with the Lithuanians to obtain the films. She also told me that some of the negatives were actually sent for safe keeping with Lithuanians outside of the ghetto and after the war, Kaudshin got them back. Her husband, Judel Zupowitz, however, was shot in March 1944, at the 9th fort. Now I will try to track down Yankele Bregman. I know that he is in Israel, but he has been out of touch with us. As soon as I will hear from him I will let you know.

Your painting is hanging in our living room and the smaller one you sent for our grand daughter, she love it very much.

I am going through the photos carefully and will try to find ways to identify them.

You keep up the good work, and continue sending me more of the photos you think are important. Concerning the photo of the 7th fort, where my brother was murdered, (No number), it is much too small to be the compound where thousands were murdered. There is a well known photo of thousands of men standing grouped together, also by Kadushin. The compound there is much larger than the one you sent me.

Good luck with Bernbaum. He wrote a very nice quote for my book. Give him my regards. In the mean time I signed a contract with a New York producer who intends to make a two hour movie of my book. Wish me luck.

Concerning the grisly photos, please do send them. They are important evidence of what the Nazis did to us.

The sign written in blood, Jews revenge is an important photo. Your suggestion is O.K. Perhaps we can find some other passages relevant to the photo.

I have to go now. Take care of your self little girl. Pola sends her love, so do I.
Solly

P.S. Send me your E mail address. I am getting connected to the internet.

Another highlight was receiving a letter from the author who wrote *The World Must Know*. Michael Berenbaum's book was the one I purchased at the campus bookstore and it was his book that started me on this unique journey in the first place. I didn't know it at the time but Michael was a respected scholar and well-known academic in Holocaust studies. As I later learned, Michael was most known for his position as the project director for the United States Holocaust Memorial Museum and many considered Michael to be one of the creators of the Museum. After Michael's position there, he later became the president of the Survivors of the Shoah Visual History Foundation, Steven Spielberg's famed archive of recorded testimonies from Holocaust survivors—therefore I was truly humbled when Michael offered to assist me in writing about my research findings. In addition, Professor Felstiner, my mentor at Stanford University, helped me gain confidence to talk about George's photography, as he invited me into his classes to share my research findings with his colleagues and students.

All in all, I was grateful that I learned as much as I did during Solly's visit to the archives but it was also a very sobering time. Although I was happy when Solly identified himself in one of George's photos and confirmed my other discoveries, joy and surprise were diminished as he pointed to the people and children who didn't survive. Moreover, Solly recalled how dangerous life was just days before moving into the ghetto when the Nazis and their Lithuanian sympathizers vandalized synagogues and destroyed lives. Also, Solly soberly recalled the grim realities of day-to-day living and explained how Jews were forcibly deported and shot. Lastly, Solly spoke about the ghetto's liquidation when the Nazis poured gasoline around the ghetto's homes and set it on fire with full knowledge that some Jews were hiding inside.

I selected the following pictures from George's photo collection because they visually encapsulated Solly's diary and spoken words to me.

Survivor testimonies from the USHMM and Solly Ganor's *Light One Candle* are in bold text unless otherwise noted. Also, my observations are in normal type, unless otherwise noted.

"Destroyed synagogue in Kovno. On June 25-26, 1941, one day after the German occupation of Kovno, Lithuanian nationalists unleashed a massive pogrom . . . Over eight hundred Jews were murdered in their homes in the most savage manner without any interference from Lithuanian or German authorities." Date: 1941. Locale: Kovno.

Photographer: George Kadish/Zvi Kadushin. Photo Credit: USHMM, courtesy of George Kadish/Zvi Kadushin.

During this time, Jewish families packed whatever they could carry, as they were forced from their homes and into the ghetto. Anyone remaining was shot. Solly and his family were no different. They had no choice but to walk through the ruins of their town to get to the ghetto. On his way to the ghetto with his family, Solly not only saw vandalized buildings and his destroyed hometown but he also witnessed murder, "**. . . the farther we proceeded the more thickly the road was strewn with corpses . . . [M]y teacher's five-year old daughter, thumb in mouth, clung to her mother's leg . . . One of the men yelled** *Fire!* **. . . "Shoot her! . . . then the leader, an older man, calmly went up to the girl and hit her over the head with his revolver. Blood spilled down her face, but she made no sound as she fell.**" (36). Moments later, Solly recognizes the body of a little girl whose back was ripped open with a shell. Her name was Dvora, and Solly's sister tutored her in Hebrew before the Germans occupied Kovno, "**Dvora was lying in the grass, a surprised look on her face. Her white dress was soaked with blood and her eyes stared unseeing at the blue sky.**" (37).

"Interior view of a synagogue vandalized by Lithuanians during the June 1941 pogrom in Kovno." Date: June 1941. Locale: Kovno.

Photographer: George Kadish/Zvi Kadushin. Photo Credit: USHMM, courtesy of George Kadish/Zvi Kadushin.

I could only imagine how frightened Solly and his family were. Also, I was in awe of George's composure. How George was able to record the destruction around him I will never know.

"Synagogue vandalized by Lithuanians during June, 1941 pogrom in Kovno. A man, covered with a prayer shawl, lies over a bench in the synagogue. A hatchet is on the bench next to him." Date: June 1941. Locale: Kovno. Photographer: George Kadish/Zvi Kadushin. Photo Credit: USHMM, courtesy of George Kadish/Zvi Kadushin.

While looking at photographs such as these, Solly said many things. His words that day in the archives room were very much like those in his diary, *Light One Candle*, when he saw a pit filled with freshly murdered people, **"I was a normal thirteen-year-old boy brought up in a sheltered environment, and suddenly I was plunged into a world where anyone who felt like it could hunt me down and kill me." "To my dying day, I will never forget.**

About thirty bodies lay pell-mell in the grave, most of them children, most of their faces frozen, were a bloody unrecognizable mess." (38).

"The city of Kovno during the German invasion." Date: 1941. Locale: Kovno Ghetto. Photographer: George Kadish/Zvi Kadushin. By courtesy of Beth Hatefutsoth, Photo Archive, Zvi Kadushin collection, Tel Aviv. (39).

Solly saw his neighbors being murdered, families cast out from their homes, and his hometown set on fire.

"German soldiers and Lithuanian civilians observe the spectacle of Lithuanian nationalists bludgeoning Jews to death at the Lietukis Garage in Kovno. June 26, 1941." (40). Date: June 26, 1941. Locale: Kovno. Origin: Zentrale Stelle des Landesjustizverwaltungen, Ludwigsburg,

Germany. By courtesy of Beth Hatefutsoth, Photo Archive, Zvi Kadushin collection, Tel Aviv.

"Lithuanians welcome German troops on the streets of Kovno." (41). Date: 1941. Locale: Kovno. Photographer: George Kadish/Zvi Kadushin. By courtesy of Beth Hatefutsoth, Photo Archive, Zvi Kadushin collection, Tel Aviv.

According to Solly, both Lithuanians and Germans forced many families out of their homes without giving Jews a chance to grab any belongings, thus many Jews were **"left with nothing."** (42).

"Property from synagogues and homes vandalized by the Lithuanians during the June, 1941 pogrom in Kovno." Date: 1941. Locale: Kovno

Ghetto. Photographer: George Kadish/Zvi Kadushin. Photo Credit: USHMM, Courtesy of George Kadish/Zvi Kadushin.

"Residents of the ghetto move . . ." Date: 1941-1942. Locale: Kovno Ghetto. Photographer: George Kadish/Zvi Kadushin. Photo Credit: USHMM, courtesy of George Kadish/Zvi Kadushin.

As Solly remembers, **"Many Jewish families were already evacuating, moving along the road carrying bundles in their arms or pushing improvised carts and baby carriages. A few had horse-drawn wagons. Lithuanians stood on both sides of the street, watching in silence as their Jewish neighbors abandoned their homes. Some of the youngsters jeered and baited the Jews; many simply went up and helped themselves to anything they liked. The Jews didn't dare object."** (43).

"Jews move their belongings into the Kovno ghetto. The man pulling the disassembled wardrobe is George Kadish's brother-in-law." Date: Circa 1941-1942. Locale: Kovno Ghetto. Photographer: George Kadish/Zvi Kadushin. Photo Credit: USHMM courtesy of George Kadish/Zvi Kadushin.

"Jews repairing or moving the ghetto fence . . ." Date: 1942-1943. Locale: Kovno Ghetto. Photographer: George Kadish/Zvi Kadushin. By courtesy of Beth Hatefutsoth, Photo Archive, Zvi Kadushin collection, Tel Aviv.

Again, George photographed exactly what Solly wrote about, ". . . we reached the ghetto's gate. Men with a yellow Star of David attached to their garments were busy working on the fence, stretching and nailing barbed wire between tall posts that were being raised . . ." (44).

"Jews transport their wood rations to their homes in the Kovno ghetto. Homes in the Kovno ghetto were heated by primitive wood-burning ovens . . . The 17,000 residents in the ghetto were supplied by the Germans with an official ration of wood, but it was woefully inadequate . . . [Kovno's Jews] were tearing down and burning fences . . ." just to keep warm. Date: 1941. Locale: Kovno Ghetto. Photographer: George Kadish/Zvi Kadushin. Photo Credit: USHMM, courtesy of George Kadish/Zvi Kadushin.

According to Solly, ". . . **December of 1941, brought one of the worst winters [our family] ever experienced. It became so cold that lying fully clothed under the blankets didn't do any good. I lay shivering the whole night, unable to warm up . . . [we had a] little wood . . . , but it was barely enough to cook the evening meal. As temperatures began dropping to four below Fahrenheit, our situation became intolerable . . . Many people in the ghetto suffered terrible frostbite. Some lost whole limbs."** (45).

"A cobbler fixes shoes in a workshop in the Kovno ghetto . . . In an attempt to find alternative work for those less able to withstand the harsh conditions of the labor brigades, the Jewish Council promoted the establishment of workshops in the ghetto." Date: 1941-1942. Locale: Kovno Ghetto. Photographer: George Kadish/Zvi Kadushin. Photo Credit: USHMM, courtesy of Instytut Pamieci Narodowej.

Getting a job was perceived as a way of staying alive. Although it was forced labor, keeping the German army supplied, as the Jewish Council reasoned, made Jews "useful," thus many jumped at the chance to work, just to live one more minute, hour, or day. As Solly recalls, **"[The Germans] needed tailors, cobblers, knitters, lock and blacksmiths, carpenters, brushmakers, and more."** (46).

"A group of Jewish men return to the ghetto after forced labor on the outside. Here they line-up at the entrance to the ghetto to be searched by German and Lithuanian guards." Date 1941-1944. Locale: Kovno Ghetto. Photograher: George Kadish/Zvi Kadushin. Photo Credit: USHMM, courtesy of George Kadish/Zvi Kadushin.

Jews caught smuggling food into the ghetto were taken to the office of the German ghetto commandant. If caught with food, Jews were often shot.

As previously mentioned, Solly almost lost his sister in this way. But Solly's sister was lucky and her life was spared only because Solly's family was able to bribe an official. Although the dangers of smuggling food was widely known, Jews were forced to smuggle, **"Hunger was one of the severest problems that faced the Kovno Ghetto. It was impossible to survive on** the daily food rations that the Germans gave to the ghetto residents. In actuality, these were starvation rations. The rations given to the Jews represented one-third of the minimum calories required for daily survival." (47).

"Patients sit in bunk beds in the Kovno ghetto hospital. At the creation of the ghetto, the Jewish council led by Dr. Elkhanan Elkes, . . . established medical clinics, an old age home and an orphanage . . . [doctors and nurses] . . . cared for a malnourished population of 17,000 with limited equipment and medicine hidden from the Germans or smuggled in on the black market. But on October 4, 1941 . . . the German police force and Lithuanian collaborators hammered . . . [the hospital doors shut] . . . and set fire to the hospital . . . killing the 67 patients and doctors inside." Date: 1941-1944. Locale: Kovno Ghetto. Photographer: George Kadish/Zvi Kadushin. Photo Credit: USHMM, courtesy of George Kadish/Zvi Kadushin.

Solly's Aunt Leena worked in the hospital and was among those who were burned alive. Solly witnessed his Aunt Leena and the others die a horrible death. While being forced by a German officer to dig a ditch with his father, Solly tried to process what was happening and was in denial for a few moments,

"Surely, I thought, hospitals are internationally protected by the Red Cross. But the German officer ordered us back out to the pit. After another hour of work, . . . two more officers joined [the other] and . . . One of them was a higher ranking officer and seemed to be in charge. 'We are behind schedule,' he said, looking at his watch. 'Lock the place up and burn it.' . . . [the Lithuanians and Germans surrounded the wooden building and began barring the doors from the outside. Several machine guns were placed around the base . . . At first all we heard was the roar of flames as they ate their way through the wood. Then we began to hear the terrible shrieks and almost inhuman cries of those inside. That blood-curdling sound will remain branded in my soul forever." (48).

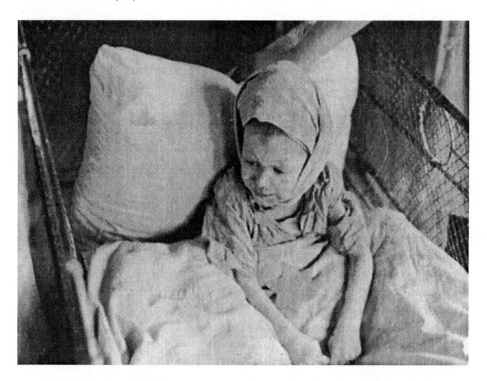

"A sick child sits in a crib in the Kovno Ghetto hospital, covered by a blanket with a Star of David." Date: 1941-1944. Locale: Kovno Ghetto. Photographer: George Kadish/Zvi Kadushin. Photo Credit: USHMM, courtesy of George Kadish/Zvi Kadushin.

"Orphanage hidden in the Kovno ghetto hospital." Date: 1941-1944. Locale: Kovno Ghetto. Photographer: George Kadish/Zvi Kadushin. By courtesy of Beth Hatefutsoth, Photo Archive, Zvi Kadushin collection, Tel Aviv.

Moments after Solly hears the screams of his Aunt Leena, the patients, doctors, and nurses, he and his father are forced to carry the remaining children and elderly patients onto trucks, which were ready to transport them to be killed, **"The most heartbreaking job was to move the orphans out of the children's ward. Little children with shaved heads led by older ones, young boys and girls whose parents were murdered by the Nazis, holding on to each other making strange noises. Many of them, out of fear, wet their pants, as their teachers and caretakers led them on their last walk on earth . . . . What had they ever done to deserve such a fate?"** (49).

While archiving George's photos of the children and ghetto's hospital, I re-read Solly's paragraphs about his family's tragedy. Quite possibly, George could have photographed the very same children Solly wrote about.

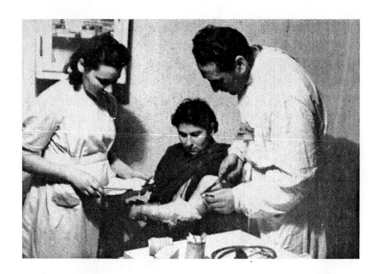

**"Dr. David Arolianski treats a patient in his clinic in the Kovno ghetto."
Date: 1941-1944. Locale: Kovno Ghetto. Photographer: George
Kadish/Zvi Kadushin. Photo Credit: USHMM, courtesy of George
Kadish/Zvi Kadushin.**

Dr. Arolianski was not killed in the hospital fire but was killed in a bunker
during the ghetto's liquidation.

**"Pictured are Avram (five years) & Emanuel Rosenthal (two years).
Emanuel was born in the Kovno ghetto . . . [they] . . . were deported
in . . . March 1944 . . . and did not survive. Their uncle, Shraga Wainer,
who had asked George Kadish to take this photograph, received a copy
of it from the photographer after the war . . ." Date: February 1944.
Locale: Kovno Ghetto. Photographer: George Kadish/Zvi Kadushin.
Photo Credit: USHMM, courtesy of Shraga Wainer.**

"Close-up portrait of the Jewish policeman, Shraga Wainer." Date: Circa 1942. Locale: Kovno Ghetto. Photographer: George Kadish/Zvi Kadushin. Photo Credit: USHMM, courtesy of Shraga Wainer.

"An elderly woman wearing a Jewish badge sits on a bed in her room in the Kovno ghetto." Date: 1941-1944. Locale: Kovno Ghetto. Photographer: George Kadish/Zvi Kadushin. Photo Credit: USHMM, courtesy of George Kadish/Zvi Kadushin.

Soon after the Nazis burned down the ghetto's hospital, Solly survives a deportation in which children and the elderly were being rounded-up by the Gestapo. In the morning, while Solly is dressing for work, he suddenly hears, **"*Achtung! Achtung!* You are all to remain in your homes. Anyone caught leaving his house will be shot! . . . Behind the car were dozens of German Gestapo . . . One of them was dragging along two little boys who lived down the street. They were in their nightgowns and their naked feet were caked with mud. Their grandmother was being pushed along by another guard . . . . My God, they were after the children and old people!"** (50).

"[They] were everywhere, breaking into houses and chasing children and old people out into the street. Once again I heard the cries of families being torn apart, the awful wailing screams of mothers whose children were torn away from them." (51).

"Portrait of Professor Simon Bieliatzkin in his room in the Kovno Ghetto. Before the war Bieliatzkin was a jurist and an expert in civil law at the University of Lithuania . . . By 1943 Bieliatzkin was suffering from severe depression and was being treated in a clandestine psychiatric unit." Date: 1943. Locale: Kovno Ghetto. Photographer: George Kadish/Zvi Kadushin. Photo Credit: USHMM, courtesy of George Kadish/Zvi Kadushin.

The ghetto's resources were incomprehensibly limited but its inhabitants and Jewish Council did as much as they could to take care of the most vulnerable.

"German soldiers prepare for a raid in the Kovno Ghetto, as some Jewish residents look on." Date: 1941-1943. Locale: Kovno Ghetto. Photographer: George Kadish/Zvi Kadushin. Photo Credit: USHMM, courtesy of George Kadish/Zvi Kadushin.

"View of the field on Demokratu Street in the Kovno ghetto . . ." Date: 1941-1944. Locale: Kovno Ghetto. Photographer: George Kadish/Zvi Kadushin. By courtesy of Beth Hatefutsoth, Photo Archive, Zvi Kadushin collection, Tel Aviv.

Miraculously, both Solly and George escaped all of the selections in the Kovno ghetto. Some selections were carried out at locations such as Demokratu, a large square in the ghetto. Throughout the ghetto's existence, the Nazis ordered Dr.

Elkahnan Elkes, head of the Jewish Council, to assemble thousands of Jews at this location where Nazi authorities selected who would live and remain in the ghetto or die by deportation to the 9th Fort where they would be shot or sent to Auschwitz to be gassed.

Solly survived a selection on October 28-9, 1941. On those two days, over twenty-eight thousand men, women, and children were forcibly assembled and stood at attention waiting for German authorities to decide who would live or die. As Solly recalls, **"Many . . . were sent to the left, some to the right. As the columns filed past and were divided, it appeared that there were more elderly people and women in the group to the right. There were also more children, including many boys my age . . . Soon, . . . families [were being torn] apart and . . . someone tried to rejoin their loved ones, but they were beaten back by the Lithuanian guards, who struck them by the butts of their rifles."** (52).

At the end of this selection, "ten thousand men, women, and children had been collected . . . and the 'lucky' ones were finally allowed to return to our homes." (53).

"Jews in the Kovno Ghetto are boarded onto trucks during a deportation action . . ." Date: October 26, 1942. Locale: Kovno Ghetto. Photographer: George Kadish/Zvi Kadushin. Photo Credit: USHMM, courtesy of George Kadish/Zvi Kadushin.

Again, while George photographed, Solly wrote, **"Hundreds of men, women, and children were being beaten and herded into the waiting trucks . . . There was no way we could get out . . . unseen . . . We had to wait until the action was over."** (54). **"The dark opening at the back of the truck was like the maw of some prehistoric monster swallowing human sacrifices."** (55). **"Finally it was over. The last trucks rumbled away with their human cargo, and there was silence. The silence of the grave."** (56). **"The monster's thirst for the blood of Jewish children seemed insatiable."** (57).

"Jewish police direct people to the assembly area in the Kovno ghetto during a deportation action . . . George captioned the back of this photo, 'Transfer to nowhere.'" Date: Circa October 26, 1943. Locale: Kovno Ghetto. Photographer: George Kadish/Zvi Kadushin. Photo Credit: USHMM, courtesy of George Kadish/Zvi Kadushin.

"The preacher, Rabbi Most, sits outside his dwelling in the Kovno Ghetto, where he awaits deportation." Date: 1942. Locale: Kovno Ghetto. Photographer: George Kadish/Zvi Kadushin. Photo Credit: USHMM, courtesy of George Kadish/Zvi Kadushin.

"Two women bid each other farewell at an assembly point . . . in the Kovno Ghetto during a deportation action . . ." Date: October 26, 1943. Locale: Kovno Ghetto. Photographer: George Kadish/Zvi Kadushin. Photo Credit: USHMM, courtesy of George Kadish/Zvi Kadushin.

"Jews are gathered at an assembly point in the Kovno ghetto during a deportation . . ." Date: Circa October 26, 1943. Locale: Kovno Ghetto. Photographer: George Kadish/Zvi Kadushin. Photo Credit: USHMM, courtesy of George Kadish/Zvi Kadushin.

"Deportation from the Kovno ghetto . . . On October 26, 1943, . . . ghetto police beg[a]n rounding up people . . . In all, 2,709 Jews were removed from the ghetto . . . Children and the elderly were shipped to Auschwitz; . . . Almost no one survived this selection." Date: 1942-1943. Locale: Kovno Ghetto. Photographer: George Kadish/Zvi Kadushin. Photo Credit: USHMM, courtesy of Yad Vashem Photo Archives.

"A pair of shoes left behind after a deportation action in the Kovno ghetto. Photographer George captioned the photo, 'The body is gone.'"
Date: Circa 1943. Locale: Kovno Ghetto. Photographer: George Kadish/Zvi Kadushin. Photo Credit: USHMM, courtesy of George Kadish/Zvi Kadushin.

"During the German occupation of the city . . . several of these forts became the sites of mass murder . . . against the Jews of Kovno . . ."
Date: After 1944. Locale: Kovno Photographer: George Kadish/Zvi Kadushin. By courtesy of Beth Hatefutsoth, Photo Archive, Zvi Kadushin collection, Tel Aviv.

When children were taken from their homes, the elderly were pulled from their hospital beds, and the ghetto's inhabitants were forced to stand at designated assembly points, such as Demokratu Square, empty trucks stood by waiting for them. Thereafter, Jews were loaded onto these flatbed trucks or forced to march to mass burial pits and shot.

In *Light One Candle*, Solly, once more, escapes and witnesses families being torn apart and hears the sounds of mass murder at the dreaded Fort, **"In the gray light of early morning, an endless column of people moved up a distant hill toward the Ninth Fort. Miles and miles of people. It wasn't as gory as many scenes I had witnessed, yet it was a thousand times worse . . . I could see these unfortunate thousands being shoved into huge graves, layer upon layer of the dead being covered with freshly dug earth . . . The numbers were so great that the death march lasted from dawn until noon . . . from almost every spot in the ghetto you could see the road that wound up the hill to the Ninth Fort, and the endless procession of the doomed moving slowly along it . . . Although the Ninth Fort was several kilometers away, we could hear the faint but unmistakable chatter of machine guns."** (58).

"Ruins of the Kovno Ghetto." Date: August 1944. Locale: Kovno Ghetto. Photographer: George Kadish/Zvi Kadushin. Photo Credit: USHMM, courtesy of George Kadish/Zvi Kadushin.

Towards the very end of the ghetto's existence, the Germans decided to rid it of its inhabitants and on July 6, 1944 demanded Jewish Council leader Elkes to issue an order directing all Jews to assemble. The Germans knew that some Jews would resist and not assemble as ordered. According to the USHMM archives, the SS were aware of the hiding spots in the ghetto, thus **"every house was blown up and the ruins [were] doused with gasoline and incinerated. Thousands were either burned to death or shot trying to flee. The fires burned for [nearly] a week, leaving a charred landscape of rubble and stone chimneys. Only approximately 100 survived the liquidation."** (59).

The camp was set aflame to smoke out those still hiding in underground bunkers. (60).

"The charred remains of Jews who were killed during the liquidation of the Kovno Ghetto." Date: August 1944-September 1944. Locale: Kovno Ghetto. Photographer: George Kadish/Zvi Kadushin. Photo Credit: USHMM, courtesy of George Kadish/Zvi Kadushin.

Solly witnessed the fiery aftermath, **"The walk to the . . . gate revealed the total devastation of the ghetto. Houses burned or gutted and corpses burned beyond recognition, many of them child size. Some had lain in the sun for several days and we had to hold our noses as we passed, the smell of burnt flesh and burnt wood was everywhere."** (61).

"A Russian officer and an elderly woman view the devastation that resulted from the razing of the Kovno Ghetto. Charred human remains are strewn among the rubble." Date: August 1944. Locale: Kovno Ghetto. Photographer: George Kadish/Zvi Kadushin. Photo Credit: USHMM, courtesy of George Kadish/Zvi Kadushin.

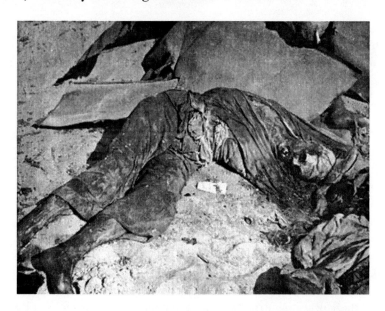

"The charred corpse of Rabbi Shmukliarski in his bunker after the razing of the Kovno ghetto." Date: July 1944. Locale: Kovno Ghetto. Photographer: George Kadish/Zvi Kadushin. Photo Credit: USHMM, courtesy of George Kadish/Zvi Kadushin.

Many died with their families and friends, while others died alone.

". . . the charred remains of Jews from the Kovno ghetto are carried on a makeshift stretcher to a mass grave." Date: August 1944. Locale: Kovno. Photographer: George Kadish/Zvi Kadushin. Photo Credit: USHMM courtesy of George Kadish/Zvi Kadushin.

Solly was only a young boy of thirteen in 1941 and George was around thirty when he took pictures of Solly and his neighbors. Despite their age difference and the different ways they chose to bear witness both Solly and George felt the same hunger pangs of starvation, witnessed horrific destruction, knew the same grief-stricken faces of those deported, and became survivors from an area where only 5% survived.

Matching the faces and locations of George's photographs with Solly's diary was an emotionally rewarding experience like no other. I felt lucky as I didn't think many people had this opportunity to learn about the ghetto and George's bravery by talking to him and seeing his work. George was committed to bearing witness to the Holocaust atrocities that occurred. According to *The World Must Know*, George is quoted as saying, "I don't have a gun. The murderers are gone. My camera will be my revenge." (62). George's legacy attests to his ingenuity, boldness, and bravery.

My bags were packed in the trunk of my car and I was bound for graduate school after a short visit with my family. I went to the archives room for one last time before leaving Los Angeles. In the six months I was there, hundreds of George's photos were dusted and measured. It was at this desk that I learned about Yehuda Zupowitz's brave deeds and made my first discovery matching Maya Gladstein's photo from George's collection to Solly's paragraph about her in his diary. I looked around the archives room and its shelves. Gone were the dog-eared, corrugated boxes. In their places now were brand-new boxes containing George's neatly filed and categorized photographs. George's photos were definitely in a better place but I missed seeing the stacked, decrepit boxes that I saw on my first day at the Simon Wiesenthal Center and Museum of Tolerance. Dust and grime were no longer on George's images; glassines and plastic sheaths now protected every piece. I'd seen hundreds of different images. I was leaving the archives room with more knowledge and experience than I'd ever imagined but I still thought of my question to George, "*Why did you rename yourself after the death prayer?*" and his bold and enigmatic response, "*I did it for the six million!*" Although I was told I'd accomplished a great deal, I still didn't know enough to understand George's answer. I didn't do enough. It was my last day in Los Angeles and I had looked at every piece there was in George's photo collection but the same question I had at the campus bookstore months ago still lingered. How was the Kaddish prayer linked to George's last name and the Jews who died during the Holocaust?

Around this time, I also decided to perform a simple on-line search for the name "Kaddish" and came up with several people who had the same or similar spelling of George's name phonetically and alphabetically. Although there were a few similarly named individuals, these people however didn't take pictures during the war as proof of Nazi crimes. While they could have changed their names for other reasons, George unequivocally and emphatically referenced the Holocaust, "*I did it for the six million!*"

I just couldn't let go of George's answer and decided to spend some time researching George's last name before going away to college. Once again I renewed the books I'd checked out before archiving George's photographs in Los Angeles and once again, I would turn to the Kaddish prayer's history. Armed with my number two pencil and yellow highlighter, I reopened my books. Learning more about the Kaddish prayer had to teach me something about George's choice to rename himself. It just had to lead me to some meaning but this time I would not just think about the Kaddish prayer in a vacuum as I did before. On the contrary, I'd consider all of George's photos, the obituary I wrote for George's daughter, and the conversations I had with George. There had to be something linking all of this together.

Re-reading paragraph after paragraph and agonizing over them finally brought some understanding. By reintroducing myself to the Kaddish prayer, I did learn that there were connections linking it to George's last name and his photographs. I learned that George's photography gave the world the possibility of hope after the Holocaust. I learned these things and more but not without first being puzzled by the complexities and challenges of the Kaddish prayer.

The Kaddish the Holocaust Created

As mentioned before, the Kaddish prayer is recited by mourners. Initially I assumed it would be sad or an elegiac prayer about the deceased but the prayer's tone is uplifting and an ultra-positive testimony of the Maker granting his will, blessing, and peace to the world He created:

> Exalted and hallowed by God's greatness
> In this world of Your creation.
> May Your will be fulfilled
> And Your sovereignty revealed
> And the whole life of the whole house of Israel
> Speedily and soon.
> And say, Amen
> May You be blessed forever
> Even to all eternity. (63).

As it turned out, I was not the only one thinking that the Kaddish's uplifting tone was unusual. One prominent author wrote, "For most Jews, the literal meaning . . . is either opaque or troubling." (64). Words such as "Blessed, praised and honored, extolled and glorified, adored and exalted" are difficult to recite for the mourner, "after all, this is the same God who ordained or permitted the death." (65). However, the recitation and repetition of such positive and honorific words are intentional. Honoring God may feel like a forced task in the wake of someone's death but the intention of the Kaddish's recitation is to steer the mourner towards life and reaffirm their relationship with God; despite overwhelming and enveloping grief, " . . . Kaddish insists that the mourner turn away from death and choose life." (66).

> May You, most Holy One, be blessed,
> Praised and honored, extolled and glorified,
> Adored and exalted above all else.
> Blessed are You.
> Beyond all blessings and hymns, praises and consolations
> That may be uttered in this world,
> In the days of our lifetime,
> And say, Amen.
> May God, Who makes peace on high,

Bring peace to all and to all Israel,
And say, Amen. (67).

My chin rested on the page and I looked at every word. Like a good driver, I interpreted each period as a stop sign at the end of a road and navigated carefully through the Kaddish. I made a full stop at the end of every "Amen" and gently paused at every comma. While I was an undergraduate at Fresno State, my professor, Dr. Stan Poss taught me to approach the reading of the written word in this literal way so that each word would receive the attention and emphasis the writer intended. For some reason he'd sometimes address me by my last name, "Gong, don't just speed through it. Pay attention to punctuation." I read it again. Also, I asked Professor Felstiner, my mentor at Stanford to recite and tape the Kaddish for me. All seven periods and thirteen commas were heard and deftly signaled every word to sway in a gentle cadence. Listing God's praise can be hard but the prayer can be comforting too, "Like a mother's heartbeat against the infant ear, [the] Kaddish makes an elemental sound—natural as rain on a wooden roof and as human as a lullaby." (68).

Typically, the Kaddish prayer addresses the mourner surviving the death of one person and the difficulty of the mourner to praise God when God is in charge of who dies and when. But praising God, as mentioned before, through the recitation of the Kaddish is necessary, because the Jewish belief, even in the event of death, extols life and the Maker.

Praising God is extremely difficult when one individual dies but it becomes almost impossible to celebrate life and God when six million die. In considering George's pictures of Holocaust atrocities and his chosen last name, Kaddish, the celebratory tone of the Kaddish prayer and its exaltation of God can become an insult to those mourning Holocaust victims. Typically, one is expected to say Kaddish for one who died of natural causes and to honor the God who permitted the death. But how is the Kaddish prayer to be considered in the context of the six million murdered? Was I disrespectful in questioning the Kaddish prayer's function given the incomprehensible loss of millions during the Holocaust? Am I supposed to accept the Holocaust as God's will? Am I to understand that God permitted the Nazis to kill innocent people?

I was frustrated and puzzled but remained committed to read more about the Kaddish and Jewish death customs. I had learned a little more and was trying to imagine what a Jewish funeral would be like. I imagined a kosher casket at a gravesite during peacetime and before the Holocaust:

A traditional casket is a plain wooden box . . . wooden pegs are preferred. Since the goal of a Jewish coffin is to permit the body to return to the earth as naturally as possible, holes are drilled in the bottom . . . [kosher caskets are] . . . crude . . . and may sell for a few hundred dollars . . . These rulings enforced a kind of democracy in death, acknowledging the elemental quality of all human beings. (69).

I also imagined a body inside the kosher casket. From what I learned the body is not extravagantly dressed but is shrouded in a "gown that has no pockets, because you can't take your possessions with you." (70). Flowers are also absent at Jewish funerals as they too can be a sign of ostentation and wealth. Again, Judaism's awareness of death's equality resurfaces. As the deceased, rich or poor, are equal before the eyes of God, so are the attending mourners. Whether attendees can afford extravagant flowers is not important and irrelevant to accepting God's will and the finality of death. Instead of flowers, each mourner carries a stone to indicate their presence and respect for the dead and will place it on the deceased's headstone.

Often flowers are present in Christian funerals but Jewish death rituals do not want mourners to be distracted or escape the realties of death. Simply, death and God's will are faced head-on, "Traditional Jewish funerals are almost stark in their simplicity. The casket is covered with a simple cloth called a pall and displayed without floral adornment. There is no soothing background music . . ." (71). Holes in an inexpensive casket and the absence of flowers are just a few of the many death traditions instructing Jews to proclaim their relationship with God during one of the most difficult times in a Jew's life. A Jew must accept both the finality and equality of death without distraction.

Food consumed during the mourning period is also specified. According to *Kaddish* by Leon Wieseltier, "Everyone may bring cakes, meat, and fish to the house of the mourner; and if a local official is present, beans and fish." (72). Symbolic also are the shapes of some foods, ". . . it is the custom to feed the mourner eggs first, because it is a thing without a mouth, to teach [us] that we have recourse only to silence with which to accept the judgment of heaven; and because it is round, like the turning wheel of the world." (73). As the existence of life and death does not have a beginning or ending and will continue as Alpha and Omega, the shape of the food itself symbolizes the cycle that will continue and never end. Indeed, a Jew's profound respect towards God's judgment is rooted in their faith and even their choices of food.

While I was learning more about the intricacies of Jewish mourning customs, I also imagined an existence without Nazism. Images of a simple kosher casket and mourners quietly placing stones on the deceased's headstone were in my mind. Then suddenly I was yanked from my reverie; I felt forced to look down at my desk. Inches away from my library books was a photocopied image from George's photo collection. It was a picture of an infant corpse face-up and atop a mound of bodies heaped on a dirt road. Surrounding her were other bodies in blood soaked clothes. Clearly there wasn't a proper burial, ceremony, or rabbi for these people. Surely no relatives attended or were able to practice Judaism's death traditions, "According to Jewish law, anyone who has lost a parent, sibling, child, or spouse recites Kaddish everyday beginning with the funeral and continuing for thirty days after the death." (74). During the pogroms of 1941, danger and chaos were everywhere. It was impossible to comply with Jewish burial customs or laws. George could have been the last person who saw many of these people before they were killed and probably thrown into a mass grave—just like the people Solly saw before moving into the ghetto. And again, I thought about George's friend, Yehuda Zupowitz, whose death was also unspeakably violent, as he was tortured and later burned. Simply, the dead were cruelly dismissed and treated without any reverence.

For four years, Kovno's Jews lived in constant fear. There were no provisions for a kosher casket, a presiding rabbi, or reverent condolences. All lived on starvation rations. The Jews Solly wrote about and George photographed didn't have the luxury of eating eggs as a symbolic gesture when someone died but only ate what they could scavenge and smuggle. As I learned from my books about Jewish death traditions, eating foods without a mouth is a symbol of silence as it is the mourners' only "recourse" "to accept the judgment of heaven." (75). In the context of the Holocaust however, am I to understand that God allowed the Holocaust to happen and the world and its Jews were expected to silently accept this? So, why would George rename himself after the death prayer—the death prayer symbolizing a Jew's faith in God when the Holocaust forced even the most faithful to question God's actions or inactions?

At this point, I doubted the Kaddish prayer's purpose and function during and after the Holocaust. By now, I thought I would have answers about George's last name but now I just had more questions and a growing sense of frustration.

A part of me felt emboldened by my research findings in Los Angeles and Solly's validation; Solly's letters and visit strengthened me. This should have been enough to fuel my energies to learn more about George's name and possible connections to Jewish death traditions but it wasn't. Sometimes reading Holocaust history and survivors' testimonies was emotionally challenging and almost always grim. Stories of salvation were few and far between and what compounded this burden now were my difficulties in understanding the Kaddish. I felt confused and increasingly alone.

When I was in the archives room, I was dusting, covering, and studying George's photos. Throughout my days and nights there, I'd often carry several, cardboard boxes that were flat, long and wide and full of George's pictures. Even though my upturned arms were fully outstretched and my fingertips barely reached the box's top edge, I never dropped a single photograph when

I carefully walked down the archives' hall. The Simon Wiesenthal Center and Museum of Tolerance also had a yeshiva for boys. At times I was in the hallway when students would change classes or run to recess. Their presence reminded me of George's commitment to educate the world about the Holocaust and how lucky these children were; they would never have to endure Solly and George's pain and experience the ghetto's horrors. These boys didn't have to wear clothing and shoes with holes in them; these boys had real toys and didn't have to make their own sleds out of fence boards and old bed frames. On one particular day, I was deep in thought but suddenly, the sounds of desks closing, doors opening, and boys laughing jolted me back to the present. The little yeshiva boys always greeted me with their smiles as they swirled around my knees on their way to the playground but their rambunctious movements keenly reminded me of the precious cargo in my arms. I reprimanded the boys softly and I held George's boxes so tight that I noticed faint, gentle red marks on the insides of my arms after I unloaded them. To some, having an image of a person is tantamount to their actual presence. Even though I am not a religious person, George's images were like living entities and I was their temporary guardian. Now, I was away from the archives room and I deeply missed carrying George's photos.

George's photos were not static, one-dimensional images but were also part of a dialogue communicating with Solly's diary. Often in the archives room, I had calm feelings of George reaching out to me from up above. Right down and through the acoustic ceiling, George provided light in the archives room and guided me to match his photographs with Solly's diary. George was like a persistent, gentle sun following me while I was away from my family and learning but now I was all alone and away from George's photos and what dominated my thoughts were questions. How relevant could this ancient Jewish prayer be after the Holocaust? Why would George deliberately rename himself after it? Did Jews attempt to practice any of these customs and rituals during the Holocaust? Did Jews think of these traditions and God differently because of the Holocaust? It was very late when I closed my books and went to bed. I had a dream about George that night,

> All around me and as far as I could see, flaxen wheat gently swayed under clouds and a blue sky. It's as if I was simply inserted in the middle of a field on a spring day. Everything was almost too beautiful and I turned around to confirm what I was seeing. I turned again just to make sure. On this turn however, I slowly looked towards my right and two people suddenly appeared. They weren't there the first time but there they were now and talking. They didn't see me as I floated towards them. Oddly, something transported me because

I didn't feel my feet and legs moving. Soundlessly, I was not only moving but was also rising as I felt the tops of the wheat brushing the bottoms of my feet. I was now hovering over these people and heard, "The Holocaust never happened. It is a fabrication of lies. It wasn't that bad!" After hearing a few minutes more of this odd and hateful conversation, I am transported away and abruptly dropped to the earth. My body, no longer weightless, flattens the wheat. I'm on my back and stand myself up to look to the sky and discover that it is no longer a beautiful blue but is growing dark. It blackens quickly and the now heavy, wet sky is flooding the wheat field. Nothing is golden anymore. Instantly, pelting rain drowns out the calm and I didn't even see or hear the disrespectful people anymore. Mud is up to my neck and my legs are scraping against tree branches and upturned roots. Just as I am about to go under the sludge, I see what looks like a baseball pitcher's mound nearby. Atop this mound is a silhouette of a man with a shovel. He's wearing a long coat and hat. I swim closer and push the mud from my eyes and now he's all that I see. I am nearing the mound and I know it's George because he's wearing a distinctive hat resembling the one he wore in a photo I'd dusted in the archives room. I get closer and it is George with this Buster Brown, newsboy-like hat atop his head. It is George and he is shoveling mud and dirt. I hear the shovel's head hitting stones and rocks and think of George's advanced age and the pain he might be feeling. My hands are now clawed onto the mound's edge and I yell, "Sir, you shouldn't be doing that. You will hurt yourself!" He stops, looks and walks over to me. He offers me his hand. I grab onto George and push myself off and up from the wet, unreliable earth. He steadies me to my feet and I regain balance. I see his eyes and gently motion towards him to take the shovel away from him. George shakes his head and then I say, "What can I do?" "How can I help?" Loudly I repeat myself as I think he doesn't hear me over the howling rain and wind. George squints his already small eyes and then bends down and grabs several stones for me to carry. George continues and my arms quickly fill. I feel the clamminess of the stones on the insides of my outstretched arms and open palms but I am not afraid of dropping them despite their slippery surface. I stiffen my arms and hands further so that I don't drop any stones and disappoint George. He finally responds to my offer for help after moments of silence, "Help me carry them." I straighten my back further to carry more stones, as George continues to dig. With my bare arms upturned and fully extended, I look at the side of his

> face and then to the sky. I am then granted a bird's eye view of the
> rain drenching us; George is still shoveling and I continue to carry
> more and more stones while standing by him.

My face and pillow were wet when I woke up. Either my tears or sweat soaked my pillow and bed's coverings. I felt stunned. I didn't know what to make of my dream or of the many stones and rocks George told me to carry. I didn't know how anything related to George's last name or the elements of the Jewish death tradition I'd learned the night before. I was uncertain about many things but what was certain was that I needed to know more and return to the library. In order to not feel so alone during my search, I tucked a photocopy of George's picture inside my notebook and taped another to my refrigerator door. I would see his image again when I returned home and ate dinner.

These photocopied images of George and my borrowed library books about the Kaddish prayer actually helped me understand my dream better. It wasn't until a month later that I came to more of an understanding. I did think about God and about the highly publicized debates scholars and rabbis had about whether God permitted the Holocaust or not. One could literally swim in all of the arguments about faith after the Holocaust and treatises about Nazi accountability. But instead of focusing on the role God could have played or did not play during the Holocaust, I thought of the many stones and rocks George gave me in my dream. Also, seeing George's photograph in my notebook was as important as seeing photographs of Solly and Avrasha Stupel in the archives room. Seeing George's photographs of Solly selling goods in the ghetto's street corner or of Avrasha playing music emphasized action and what they were doing. Similarly, having an image of George in my kitchen helped me to squarely focus on his actions. In my dream, George gave me stones to hold while he was shoveling and said, "Help me carry them." George's actions and his request helped me understand that each photograph I carried in the archives was like a symbolic stone paying respect to those he photographed in the Kovno ghetto.

As I'd learned from my books about Jewish death rituals, a stone left at a grave is a symbol indicating a mourner's visit and respect for the mourned. On a literal level, a stone endures and is long-lasting. As flowers at a gravesite may wither from the sun and its petals may be torn by the wind, a single stone is relatively immovable and impervious to climate. Whereas a change in weather can wash away a visitor's flowers and therefore eliminate all signs of visitation, George's photograph of one person, like a symbolic stone, irrefutably indicates George's presence or his "visit" to them. These photographs, like stones at an Orthodox funeral, symbolize the permanence of not only George's presence to his subjects, as he is the person who literally activated his camera's shutter but

George's photographs also provide permanence for his subjects' very existence. During the Holocaust, it was uncertain who was going to live or die as people were murdered on such unprecedented levels. Perhaps, it is because of this uncertainty that George left the world photographs—a permanent chronicle and therefore a permanent marker memorializing himself, and both the living and dead in the ghetto.

George Kaddish: Kovno's Son and Europe's Son

This concept of memorializing both the mourned and the mourner is, I believe, ultimately realized in George's photography. As long as George's photos are protected and preserved in Los Angeles, Israel, and Washington, D.C., his work is an everlasting testament of life and death in Kovno's ghetto. George however enlarged his role in bearing witness by linking his entire identity with his actions during the Holocaust. By intentionally renaming himself after the death prayer, George's photography and his persona have been transformed into a symbolic Kaddish.

These realizations about George's last name became stronger as I returned to my library books and learned that the Kaddish prayer is not only a doxology or listing of God's praise but is also an individual. "Sons were referred to as 'my Kaddish' or as a 'Kaddishl,' and people who had no sons sometimes hired men to say the prayer after they died." (76). However, women in the more liberal practice of Judaism can also say the Kaddish, "According to Jewish law, anyone who has lost a parent, sibling, child, or spouse recites Kaddish . . ." (77). In one touching account, a rabbi consoles a grieving mother who loses a very young son, "You know, now you are the Kaddish. Usually the child is the Kaddish for the parents, but you are his Kaddish." (78). Children are expected to outlive their parents and a Kaddish was traditionally a son who was expected to say the death prayer for his parents but because of the boy's premature death, the only one left to say the Kaddish for him was his mourning mother, thus the mother became her son's Kaddish.

Even though the rabbi's counseling and the young man's death have nothing to do with the Holocaust, the meaning of Kaddish and becoming one resonates with George's selection of 'Kaddish' as his last name because the traditional expectation of who a Kaddish is changes. Outside the historical context of the Holocaust, a Kaddish to a father is his son and in some cases when the parent outlives her child, the mother is the son's Kaddish as mentioned above. The latter predicament is unfortunate but this happens, especially when infant and child mortality rates were higher generations ago. Still, this is considered an exception. Within the confines of the Holocaust however, a Kaddish, in many cases, became any family member who was alive or simply available. As traditionally expected and as stated before, it is the younger who is supposed to be the Kaddish for his dead elder. But during the Holocaust, and as George's images and Solly's diary chronicle, the Nazi thirst for Jewish blood could not be quenched, thus family members of all ages were murdered every second of every day. Nazi hate was indifferent to the generational and mortal order of families; sons and daughters died before the very eyes of their parents and grandparents. A grandfather could become the Kaddish to his infant granddaughter.

In cases when it was assumed that the dead had no family at all, Jews during the Holocaust became a Kaddish to those unrelated or unknown to them. In one section of Solly Ganor's book, Solly speaks about his friend Zelig who had already lost his mother and father, "Zelig was a quiet boy. He came from a small town where his entire family was murdered . . ." (79). Later, Solly says the death prayer for him. According to Solly's written account, Zelig mistakes a hunched figure as his uncle and runs from a hiding place to greet the old man, despite the presence of a Nazi guard. As the German sees the boy approach, he beats up both the man thought to be 'Uncle Moshe' and Zelig at the construction site where cement is being poured. During the scuffle, Zelig, the old man, and the guard fall into the pit; all three are suffocated by the fresh cement and instantly entombed. Shortly after, Solly says the Kaddish both for Zelig and the old man who was mistaken for Zelig's uncle, "On the way back I mourned my friend Zelig and recited Kaddish for him in my head. Also for the man he called his uncle . . ." (80). Because Zelig was the last remaining member in his family and it was evident that Uncle Moshe was also alone and without family or freinds, Solly became the Kaddish for both. During peacetime it is true that, "Many people choose to say Kaddish for people outside their immediate nuclear family . . ." and "[t]he tradition does not prohibit anyone from widening the circle," as "[f]riends and lovers" are included as well, but in Solly's world, the deceased's Kaddish was no longer a relative or a specific, designated person—best friend, cousin, or significant other. (81). On the contrary, a Kaddish could become anyone who was simply alive or around at the time of anyone's death.

Becoming a Kaddish to a dead friend with no surviving family members and a stranger right at the time of their deaths is grim. But it is unimaginable to become a Kaddish to one's own mother when it is not confirmed that she is even dead. In *Light One Candle*, Solly's father agonizes over the well-being of his spouse, Rebecca. Solly's father does not know if his beloved wife is alive but he reflexively says the Kaddish prayer for Rebecca as he had a premonition of her death and doesn't know if anyone was the Kaddish for her, "I was there. Don't ask me how." "We might as well say Kaddish, son," and [he] started chanting the ancient prayer for the dead." (82). Even though it is "forbidden to start mourning until after the moment of death," Solly's father expects the very worst and preemptively recites the death prayer, thus both father and son become the Kaddish for both wife and mother. (83).

As it was widely understood that others were going to meet certain, fast approaching death, Jews themselves became their own Kaddish because it was assumed that death could visit them at any time. Omnipresent death was felt not only in Lithuania but Poland. According to Elie Wiesel in *Night*, the Kaddish's grim recitation was openly heard, "Everybody around us was weeping. Someone began to recite the Kaddish, the prayer for the dead." (84). The Final Solution's mission of eliminating every Jew impacted every village, town, and city where there were Jews—not just in Poland and Lithuania. The spontaneous round-ups of Jews, countless deportations to concentration camps, and numerous firing squads created a chaotic environment of death where anything could happen to anyone at anytime. Before the Holocaust, the Kaddish was a designated person who said it for the deceased but during the Holocaust, Jews became their own Kaddish as they didn't have time to select a particular person and automatically anticipated their own deaths every minute. As a result of the unprecedented event called the Holocaust, the definition of the Kaddish took on a new meaning in this unprecedented way. As Elie Wiesel said, "I don't know whether, during the history of the Jewish people, men have ever before recited Kaddish for themselves." (85).

Pre-emptive recitation of the Kaddish prayer and the reflexive assumption of the Kaddish role were apt responses to a world in which the living were already dead. In Solly's diary, he speaks of returning to the ghetto after escaping a deportation and mourning the loss of his friends and neighbors,

> Everywhere I went I heard the terrible lament of people who had lost their families. I felt guilty to be alive. Yet I had very little doubt that my turn would soon come. The only reason the rest of us were still alive was because they couldn't murder thirty thousand people at a time. In one house after another I heard people saying Kaddish. The dead praying for the dead. (86).

Although I've specifically highlighted the testimonies of Solly Ganor and Elie Wiesel, accounts like theirs were all too common during the Holocaust. Thousands of stories are not known simply because people did not survive to tell them. With that said, George did unfortunately witness similar accounts, such as the ones told in *Night* and *Light One Candle*. George witnessed the rapid decimation of not only Kovno's Jews but the world's Jews. Perhaps it is because of these tragic witnessings that George changed his last name from Kadushin to Kaddish, "I did it for the six million!" George intentionally became the Kaddish for not only Kovno's Jews but for all of Europe's Jews. It is inconsequential if George was a parent, sibling, child, spouse or best friend to any of the six million he photographed. Symbolically, George became the Kaddish to the six million because it was not known if there would be any Jews left in the world. "In liberated Lithuania, only 8,000 to 9,000 Jews remained from the prewar population of 235,000. More than 95 percent of Lithuanian Jewry had been destroyed." (87). This is the Kaddish the Holocaust created; a hellish world in which simultaneously, the living became the dead, the mourner became the mourned, and the old wept for their young.

George's choice of becoming a Kaddish is symbolic and changing his last name to Kaddish is an unforgettable symbol but equally powerful are George's photographs of the Kovno ghetto and its Jews. Arguably, George's images are a Kaddish too. According to *Wrestling with the Angel*, it is the Kaddish's "responsibility to keep the memory of the dead person alive, to not forget, [and] not let others forget." (88). Again, the rabbi's counseling is not about the Holocaust but about the mother's identity and duty to her son who died prematurely, "Usually the child is [the] Kaddish for the parents but you are his Kaddish." (89). True, George's photography, in a literal sense is not an immediate relative like the grieving mother or even a living entity. However, George's images are a figurative Kaddish because his photos uphold the "responsibility to keep the memory of the dead person alive, to not forget, [and] not let others forget." (90). It is not important or certain if George literally said the Kaddish prayer or became a designated Kaddish to any of the Jews during the Holocaust but George's photography unequivocally and tangibly demonstrates that he and his photographic chronicle, as a Kaddish, metaphorically assumed the traditional honor of keeping the memory of the six million alive.

Thus far, what has been discussed is George bearing witness to the *deaths* of the six million. However what has not been covered is George bearing witness to the *lives* of the six million. Life, as Judaism emphasizes always takes precedence over death, ". . . the bottom line is startlingly clear. In words and through practice, Kaddish insists that the mourner turn away from death and choose life." (91). Just as George fulfilled the role of the Kaddish for the dead, he also remained faithful to Judaism by honoring life through his photography.

On my desk were George's photocopied images. Yes, there were pictures of body parts, charred corpses, and destroyed buildings burned beyond recognition but there were also photos of children smiling and playing in the snow, musicians practicing, and the most touching of all, a mother holding a baby in her arms. "After the Germans issued a decree in July 1942 making pregnancy illegal and punishable by death, few children were born in the ghetto." (92). The Nazis hunted for children both inside and outside a woman's womb. For two days (March 27-8, 1944), the Nazis, in their "Kinderakzion" deportation, searched "every single attic, . . . basement, cave, and tunnel" for children, "whom they dragged out to be annihilated." (93). However, Kovno's Jews resisted and George's photos show life in the ghetto.

Children existed in the ghetto but there weren't many. According to the USHMM archives, **"Approximately 10,000 children and youth below the age of 20 moved into the Kovno ghetto in August 1941. Within a few months almost half of them (4,400) . . . perished [on] . . . October 28, 1941." Date: not recorded. Locale: Kovno Ghetto. Photograher: George Kadish/Zvi Kadushin. Published Source: USHMM archives and USHMM *Hidden History of the Kovno Ghetto.***

"Portrait of two young boys with a milk can." Date: 1941. Locale: Kovno Ghetto. Photographer: George Kadish/Zvi Kadushin. Photo Credit: USHMM, courtesy of George Kadish/Zvi Kadushin.

Children not only faced spontaneous deportations but also suffered from malnutrition, typhus, and rickets.

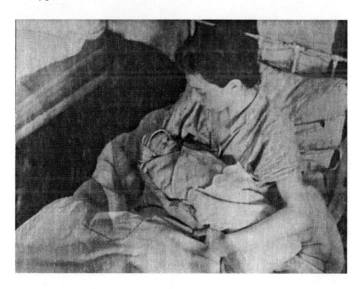

"A mother cradles her newborn baby in the Kovno ghetto hospital. The child is swaddled in a blanket with a Star of David." Date: 1941-1944. Locale: Kovno Ghetto. Photographer: George Kadish/Zvi Kadushin. Photo Credit: USHMM, courtesy of George Kadish/Zvi Kadushin.

The Nazis did everything they could to control the population of Jews hence, pregnancy was considered a capital crime in 1942, "**. . . giving birth in the ghetto is forbidden under punishment of death. Every pregnancy must be terminated. Termination of pregnancies will be carried out in the hospital . . .**" (94). It was understood that mothers would be shot if their babies were not aborted. Jews did their best to hide pregnancies and find hiding places for their children.

"Musical performance in the Kovno ghetto." Date: August 1942-March 1944. Locale: Kovno Ghetto. Photographer: George Kadish/Zvi Kadushin. Photo Credit: USHMM, courtesy of George Kadish/Zvi Kadushin.

Despite the grim realities of the ghetto, music raised "**. . . the level of morale in the ghetto.**" (95).

"Children playing in the snow, on sleds improvised from boards and broken pieces of other objects." Date: 1941-1943. Locale: Kovno Ghetto. Photographer: George Kadish/Zvi Kadushin. Photo Credit: USHMM, courtesy of Yad Vashem.

Date: not recorded. Locale: Kovno Ghetto. Photographer: George Kadish/Zvi Kadushin. Source Credit: USHMM archives.

Children did their best to have a childhood in the ghetto.

I did see the tattered and ill-fitting clothing of the children. I did see the star on the baby's blanket and opera singer's dress. Most heartbreakingly, I saw the frailty of these children. I saw all of this but I also saw life and hope. Despite the grim realities of the ghetto, Kovno's Jews held concerts and its children played with make-shift sleds during the harsh winters. Solly and his friends even hid books upon the threat of death,

> . . . the Germans ordered all books in the ghetto to be turned over to the authorities. Anyone caught with books after the deadline would be executed . . . [but that didn't stop us, our] final load consisted of . . . Tolstoy, Lermontov, Dostoyevsky, Turgenev, Pushkin, Gogol—the thoughts, passions, ideals, and feelings of literary giants were in those books. (96).

"Children pose next to a wagon filled with Jewish books . . . In February 1942, . . . the Germans executed the Buecheraktion (Book Action), during which ghetto residents were forced to hand over all books and printed matter in their possession upon penalty of death." Date: February 1942. Locale: Kovno Ghetto. Photographer: George Kadish/Zvi Kadushin. By courtesy of Beth Hatefutsoth, Photo Archive, Zvi Kadushin collection, Tel Aviv.

In *Light One Candle*, Solly witnesses his teacher, Mr. Edelstein, paying the ultimate price for possessing a book, **"Suddenly the Lithuanian began** shouting 'What's this you got hidden there, Jew boy? A book? And in your heathen language too . . ." "I stood frozen in horror as . . . the guard began beating my teacher . . . With that I found my feet and started running. I was turning into a side street when I heard a shot. I looked back to see Mr. Edelstein fall to his knees. The German put his pistol to his head and fired again, and Mr. Edelstein fell over and lay still." (97). Despite danger, Solly and his friends still smuggled and read books as it kept their minds off of malnutrition, murder, and torture, "[I] escaped . . . grief by reading." (98). "[Books] helped make a terror-filled world a little more bearable." (99).

George's images of Kovno's people—these grandfathers, grandmothers, fathers, mothers, sisters, brothers, aunts, uncles, cousins, and even the boys hiding and reading books—all attempted to live and thrive despite the death surrounding them.

For some reason, I put all of George's images away except for two: a photocopy of a children's nursery and another of a woman cradling her baby were both now on my desk. George's images almost appeared too common and I was struck by their apparent normalcy. Doing "normal" things was extraordinary in the ghetto.

I dug deeper in my books and found out that much study is devoted to this very subject of doing very normal things, such as having children, in places like Kovno, ". . . [where] . . . life was so degrading and dehumanizing that it defies the imagination of anyone who did not actually himself share in the experience." (100). Every attempt to ". . . degrade . . . to the extent of losing . . . the last vestiges of . . . humanity . . ." was exploited by the Germans. (101). There were people who literally disintegrated under these circumstances and they were called "Moslems." (102). According to Rabbi Bercovits, a leading Talmudic scholar, "Moselms" were concentration camp prisoners who were broken in spirit and unable to express any emotion. The Nazis' mission of dehumanizing each Jew was absolute but their goal was not entirely reached. Miraculously, some Jews were still able to express emotions and therefore remain 'human' despite being treated worse than animals. As George's photographs show, some mothers did have children in the ghetto despite the Nazis' attempts to forcibly sterilize women. The Germans enforcing the pregnancy prohibition treated Jewish women like cattle requiring sterilization. However, George's lens grant us a vision of a Jewish woman's soul revealing very human emotions: to love and care for a child.

In introducing Rabbi Bercovits' theory, I discussed the existence of 'Moslems.' It is not my intent, nor the rabbi's, to imply that those who were able to have babies were strong and those who were not were weak, emotionless, or inhuman. On the contrary, the discussion's intention was to highlight cases in which the totality of Nazi cruelty was absolute.

As discussed, having children is a normal, yet life changing rite of passage for many women in our present-day world but in the context of the ghetto this ordinary act was truly extraordinary. But there were many other occurrences in the ghetto that were not considered as life changing as having a baby, yet these activities were still out of the ordinary. Doing things such as singing, reading, and just having fun were also considered extraordinary. As we've seen, George's pictures show Kovno's Jews doing things we often take for granted. Kids are snow sledding and carrying book bags in several of his photos. Boys are even smiling and grinning. If I didn't know the origin of George's pictures and had found them in a footlocker sold at a garage sale, these idyllic scenes could have been from someone's grandfather in Iowa where he played with his boyhood friends in the snow. The photos' inscriptions could have read, 'Des Moines, Winter of 1941' but this was Kovno, Lithuania during the Holocaust. By doing these normal, everyday things in the ghetto, Jews were not subhuman as the Nazis considered and treated them but in fact were superhuman despite death and murder around them. George Kaddish, Yehuda Zupowitz, Maya Gladstein, Misha Hoffmeckler, and Avrasha Stupfel, and all the photographed people were extraordinary by trying to live ordinary lives during the Holocaust.

The word, 'resistance,' often evokes images of a highly organized faction fighting against a majority or a large group of armed people having a unified mission of overthrowing a regime. But in the context of the Holocaust and George's pictures of the Kovno ghetto, resistance was considered living life as normally as one could despite intolerable conditions. Furthermore it meant fighting to stay "human" despite being treated sub-humanly. George's subjects are not exhibiting resistance in grand, sweeping ways. On the contrary, George chronicled a type of psychological resistance and captured quiet moments epitomizing a mother's love or a singer's expression of music. There is dignity and even mischief despite danger. In recalling George's photograph of the Jewish boys surrounding a wagonload of books, one boy is sticking his tongue out while others are smiling.

Resistance is also revealed in gestures showing grace and sacrifice. As one survivor recalled:

> Ilse, who worked on the day shift, came back by noon . . . She turned away from me so that I could not see what she was doing, and dug into her pocket. "I have brought you a present!" she announced triumphantly. There on a fresh leaf was one red, slightly mashed, raspberry. (103).

Even though Ilse didn't smuggle in a bag of groceries or even a loaf of bread, Ilse's single raspberry is proof that Nazi cruelty didn't destroy a Jew's humanity, ". . . in the act of gift-giving, [when] life itself is given, . . . [Ilse's raspberry] offers no real nourishment, but it represents . . . the feeding of one's inner being . . ." (104). In an environment like the Kovno ghetto or a concentration camp where there are unrelenting acts denying and destroying humanity, giving a raspberry, reading a book, or seeing a child's smile are "moment(s) of human joy and sharing, and then life itself becomes the gift snatched from the enemy's grip." (105).

In our present-day world, we may simply consider this woman's gift as a humble, kind gesture but in George's world, her act epitomizes true greatness. Rabbi Berkovits would agree and also finds Ilse's actions both awe-inspiring and confounding,

> Inexplicable is the fact that the overwhelming majority of the inmates did not surrender their humanity to the very end; that, on the contrary, there were . . . sublime heights of self-sacrificial heroism and dignity of human compassion and charity. This was the true mystery of the ghettos and the death camps. (106).

George's entire chronicle captures these moments of resistance. George didn't use an armed weapon to resist and defy Nazi tyranny but used a homemade camera chronicling Jews living and surviving the best they could. On record, living normally despite intolerable conditions was the ". . . Jewish routine, . . ." (107). George's images show that Kovno's Jews were responding to the world that was ". . . bent on crushing the Jew . . ." (108). If anyone questioned the humanity of the Jewish people, George's photography is a bold testament of their resistance to inhumanity.

Faith in God and Life
No Matter What

George's photography shows Jews keeping the commandments; the essence of practicing Judaism. They went about their normal lives and they also attempted to fortify their covenant with God by obeying His laws.

"An adult and a child, read a Yiddish sign propped-up against a wall in the ghetto. The sign reads: *Jews! Donate old winter clothing and footwear that you don't need to the poor and naked. Give generously.***"** **Date: 1941-1944. Locale: Kovno Ghetto. Photographer: George Kadish/Zvi Kadushin. Published Source: USHMM** *Hidden History of the Kovno Ghetto.*

George photographed a poster outside the ghetto's Welfare Office asking for donations of used clothing for those in greater need. Even when Kovno's Jews had very little, performing mitzvah such as *tzedakah* was still expected.

According to Rabbi Ted Falcon, founder of Makom Ohr Shalom, a synagogue for Jewish meditation in Los Angeles, there are around 400 laws for contemporary Jews to follow. All told, "there are 613 total commandments" but because some of the laws are not applicable to modern society (for instance finding a temple for animal sacrifice), "over 200 of them can no longer be observed." (109).

Of these commandments, there are good deeds or mitzvot and ". . . consist of ritual as well as ethical acts . . . ," such as philanthropy or charity. (110). The commandment appearing in George's photograph of the sign promotes *tzedakah* which is commonly understood as 'charity' but more specifically, as there is no Hebrew word for 'charity,' *tzedakah* literally means 'justice.' This sign commands Jews to give to the very poor in the ghetto because a Jew is commanded to right a wrong in an imperfect and unjust world, "Helping to repair the world is a way to translate grief into healing and justice, *tzedek*." (111). *Tzedakah* is one of the most important commandments of the estimated 400 laws. (112). The caption in *The Hidden History of the Kovno Ghetto* reads, "Poster for the Welfare Office asking for donations of used clothing for those in greater need." (113). It was difficult to just survive the ghetto but it becomes almost inconceivable that Jews expected Jews to honor the law of *tzedakah* during the Holocaust. Nonetheless, George's photograph shows Jews giving charitably even when they had very little themselves.

As the very poorest of Kovno's Jews dedicated themselves to feeding and clothing the most impoverished in the ghetto, extreme lengths were also taken to preserve their cultural and religious identity, Jews ". . . concealed ceremonial objects . . . [such as] sacred texts and scrolls." (114). Hiding objects was a perpetual concern. For instance, the written text required for the Jewish holiday of Purim, such as the story of Esther, ". . . was hidden in the ghetto and protected from the confiscations." (115). According to *The Hidden History of the Kovno Ghetto*, on February 27, 1942, the Nazi edict stated, ". . . All ghetto inhabitants are required to turn in all of their books, regardless of content or language." (116). Those who didn't comply were usually shot on the spot. But when these items were stolen from them, Kovno's Jews didn't give up. On the contrary, they took risks and made their own ceremonial objects from anything they could find.

For instance, it is customary that Jews wear special garments with *tzitzit*. Physically, *tzitzit* resembles fringes and is a symbol of God's 613 commandments. In the third century, Rabbi Simlai taught that there were 613 commandments given by God in the Torah (also called *taryag mitzvot*). (117). The sum of 613 comes from two figures. The first amount corresponds to the number of positive laws, which is 248; for example, "Honor they mother and father." (118). The second figure corresponds to the number of negative laws, which is 365; for example, "Thou shall not steal." (119). The importance of living the commandments can't be overstated, "The biblical Book of Numbers states that

Jews must wear *tzitzit* (fringes) at the corners of their garments to help them remember God and the commandments." (120). Others may take a more militant approach to remind observant Jews of their obligations to God, ". . . wearing the *tzitzit* is like wearing an army uniform; when you wear one, you're very aware of your allegiances." (121). Simply *tzitzit* is a both a garment and mnemonic device, as it wraps around the Jew reminding him always to be faithful to all of God's laws, both negative and positive.

Tzitzit is just one example of the importance of cultural artifacts in a Jew's daily life. Undoubtedly, articles such as *tzitzit* were confiscated but despite the Nazis' decree, Kovno's Jews found a way to make them from scratch when there were no *tzitzit* ". . . available in the ghetto." (122). Meir Abelow, an inhabitant of the Kovno ghetto, resisted the Nazis by stealing ". . . some strands of wool, . . ." and making this into *tzitzit*. (123). Grateful to Abelow, Jewish boys in the ghetto were also mindful of God's commandments to wear *tzitzit* ". . . at all times, so that if they were God forbid taken to be killed they might be buried wearing [them] in accord[ance] with Jewish custom." (124). Faith and obedience to the Bible existed despite death. In Numbers 15:38-39, it is clearly stated,

> Speak unto the children of Israel, and bid them that they make them fringes in the borders of their garments throughout their generations, and that they put upon the fringe of the borders . . . And it shall be unto you for a fringe, that ye may look upon it and remember all the commandments of the Lord, and do them; . . . (125).

While reading about Meir Abelow's boys, I thought about George's photograph of the dead man hunched over a bench. This photo was taken during the pogrom of 1941 when Solly and his family were moving into the ghetto before it was sealed. All around the man were tossed prayer shawls and books in a desecrated synagogue. Again, what I was seeing in George's photographs corresponded to what I was reading. The Nazis and their sympathizers killed Jews anytime, anywhere—even at the very site of worship. It is inconsequential whether Meir Abelow's boys saw George's picture, if they knew the man in the photo, or if a neighbor of theirs was killed in this way. More importantly, wearing *tzitzit* as commanded and before they could be "taken to be killed" indicates their anticipation of being murdered in an environment very much like the one George photographed. Meir Abelow's boys prepared themselves to die as Jews and seemed to rehearse for a grim fate possibly met by their families, friends, and neighbors. In Kovno, some Jews adapted and stitched their own religious artifacts from scratch despite dangers. As George's photographs attest, Jews invented ways to practice their religion and at the same time prepared for a violent end.

Some Jews figured out how to honor God and His Commandments on their own, while some of the faithful sought wise counsel from rabbis. Rabbi Oshry, a Lithuanian Jew who survived the Kovno ghetto, was an active rabbi during the Holocaust. Rabbi Oshry issued *responsa* or in translation, "answers" to the questions of the devout who wanted to stay true to the practice of their faith. Because of their impoverishment and ghettoization, Jews couldn't adhere to the strict dietary and other rabbinic laws as they did in peacetime, therefore they sought guidance from Rabbi Oshry for approved alternatives. Options were few and decisions were difficult to make but Rabbi Oshry's responsa always chose life over death or sustenance over starvation. In fact, the ". . . Torah says 'Choose Life,' . . . [which is] . . . the religious principle of preserving human life (*p'kuach nefesh*), and is considered a primary mandate." (126). Starvation was a reality and it was accepted that keeping kosher was not as important as staying alive. Another survivor from the Kovno ghetto writes, "Before the war our house was kosher and we did not eat bacon. But under . . . ghetto conditions, food was food . . . We could not afford to be so particular. Bacon was the cheapest and most nutritious." (127). Rabbi Oshry would have approved.

"Portrait of Rabbi Ephraim Oshry studying a tractate of the Talmud, after the liberation . . . He became a leading religious authority in the ghetto . . . In the ghetto he offered clandestine classes in Talmud . . . and took care of Kovno's library . . . until the book confiscation of February 1942." Date: 1944. Locale: Lithuania. Photographer: George Kadish/Zvi Kadushin. Source: Yad Vashem Photo Archives.

Rabbi Oshry's presence in the ghetto was a symbol of humanity in a place where there was little hope, "**. . . the people . . . in the midst of the blackest darkness, kept the eternal lamp of Torah burning. Despite the German defilement everywhere around them, they always managed to reserve a small corner for Torah, for sanctity, for purity.**" (116). After the war, Rabbi Oshry settled in New York, where he became a rabbi of the Beth Hamedrash Hagadol on the Lower East Side and became the author of *Responsa from the Holocaust* and *The Annihilation of Lithuanian Jewry.*

"According to Rabbi Ephraim Oshry, the boys are students in the religious Tifferes Bachurim school." Date: 1941-1943. Locale: Kovno Ghetto. Photographer: George Kadish/Zvi Kadushin. Photo Credit: USHMM, courtesy of George Kadish/Zvi Kadushin.

Questions to Rabbi Oshry and his *responsa* became more difficult as ghetto conditions worsened and the Holocaust continued. This also became true in other camps and ghettos throughout Europe,

> . . . the considered rulings of Jewish law given by rabbis . . . [were] in
> response to never-before-imagined questions. May a father purchase
> his son's escape from the ovens, knowing that the quotas will be met
> and another child will die in his place? May a Jew in the Kovno ghetto

recite the morning benediction—Blessed are you, O Lord, Who has not made me a slave? How should one celebrate Passover, the festival of freedom in a concentration camp? (128).

Once, Rabbi Oshry was asked whether a critically ill Jew in the ghetto's hospital was expected to fast on Yom Kippur. According to Rabbi Oshry's *Responsa from the Holocaust*, many sick Jews did observe Yom Kippur but were advised not to do so as it would jeopardize their life, ". . . and he shall live by them, not that one should die as the result of fulfilling the commandments." (129). It was also said, "One may break every Jewish law—eat pork, work on the Sabbath—if it might save a life or promote the healing of someone who is ill." (130).

One of the more difficult *responsa* involved, yet again, the difficult choice between fulfilling God's law and staying alive. According to Rabbi Oshry, his colleague, Reb Efrayim Mordechai Yaffe faced a grim situation. Reb Yaffe needed to know if it was permissible to eat in the same room with a corpse. According to Reb Yaffe's account, an old man died of sickness and malnutrition and Reb Yaffe discovered him upon return to his house in the ghetto. Traditionally, it is prohibited for a corpse to be in the presence of people. Certainly one could not eat in front of the body but it was impossible for Reb Yaffe to eat by leaving his room and house because it was dangerously cold and the ghetto's mandatory curfew, if broken, was punishable by death. Moreover, his house was overcrowded with other Jews, thus he could not ask them to jeopardize their health and lives by asking them to leave either. How could they all survive and still respect the dead?

The tradition and Jewish custom of honoring (*kevodHa-met*) and caring (*taharah*) for the dead, forbids public viewing, "All branches of Judaism agree that, out of respect for the body, . . . there should not be a public viewing." (131). Promptly, Rabbi Oshry describes the situation and later declares his responsa to Reb Yaffe's predicament, "because of the great cold, it was impossible for them to eat their meal outside; nor could they forego their breakfast because it was not possible to survive a day of slave labor without food. Might they be allowed to eat in the presence of the corpse?" (132).

However difficult, unfortunate, and morbid Reb Yaffe's situation was, Rabbi Oshry's *responsa* again honors the precept to 'Choose Life,'

> In that case, where it was impossible for the unfortunates to eat their meal in any place other than the room with the corpse in it, I relied on the authorities who recommend that a screen be put up between the dead body and the diners while they eat. But if that too were impossible, I ruled that they should eat in the presence of the body, for not to eat would endanger their lives.(133).

Rabbi Oshry's *responsa*, the testimonies from Kovno's Jews, and George's pictures reinforce the Torah's precept to 'Choose Life' and reveal a Jew's deep commitment to faith and life no matter what the conditions are. Furthermore, these examples show the conflict Jews faced everyday during the Holocaust. To choose between sustaining one's life and honoring God's laws was a constant reality but a Jew's choices, however limited, emphasized the fundamental importance of actions preserving one's life over faith.

George's Kaddish:
A Legacy of Resistance and Our
Responsibility

George's photography recorded the daily lives of Kovno's Jews. More importantly however, George recorded actions demonstrating the Jews' courage to resist death and inhumanity by going through the daily routines of life and practicing their faith. George's courage to record the lives of Kovno's Jews matches the courage the Jews had in attempting to live and thrive the best way they could. I often wondered how well George knew his subjects or if he had anything in common with those he photographed besides being Jewish and forced to live in the ghetto. I will never know because I didn't get the chance to ask George before he died but what is certain is that both George and his subjects left the world a legacy of resistance. Activities such as taking pictures, as well as playing music, and reading the Torah were all punishable by death. Even though all of these activities were as different as the people who played a violin or secretly studied God's 613 commandments at night, George and all of his subjects, intentional or not, were brought together by their common resistance against their captors. Each picture captures a person's humanity despite the inhumanity surrounding him. As previously mentioned, to those who considered Kovno's Jews and all of Europe's Jews sub-humans, George's work is an irrefutable pictorial of humanity. George's chronicle of resistance gives the world hope that humanity survives and continues to despite intolerance and hate.

George's photography as well as the people he photographed give us this truth now and forever.

"A teacher reviews a religious text with two boys in the Landsberg displaced persons' camp." Date: 1946-1947. Locale: Landsberg. Photographer: George Kadish/Zvi Kadushin. Photo Credit: USHMM, courtesy of George Kadish/Zvi Kadushin.

A photograph says something about its subjects but also reveals much about the person who took it. After all the camps were liberated, George photographed individuals who still believed in God and Judaism. More telling though, George's act of photographing the teacher and his two students reveal that George didn't necessarily have to be a religious person to celebrate the strength of the Jews to continue to live and live spiritually despite the Holocaust. A historian commented upon the state of Judaism in the post-Holocaust world, "After Auschwitz, there is no faith, so whole as a faith shattered, . . . in the ovens." (134). On the contrary, faith exists: George's photographs of Jews committing acts of *tzedakah* (justice) during and after the Holocaust shows that the *hatikvah* (hope) of *tikkun* (healing) resides in people then and now (135).

Doing is Becoming . . .
Becoming is Doing

The Holocaust may have changed the traditional expectation of who a Kaddish could be and the way we interpret resistance during the Nazi era. But what has not changed is the strength of a Jew's *mitzvah*, "We have firepower called *mitzvot*: we act out our Jewish values." (136). Understanding Judaism, as mentioned before, is secondary to the actions a Jewish person takes. George didn't have to fully understand the implications of naming himself after the death prayer, Jewish death traditions, or the symbolic significance of his photography. Most importantly, George's actions fulfilled the *mitzvah* commanding the mourner to ". . . not forget, [and] not let others forget . . ." (137). In some ways, George's unprecedented chronicling activities goes beyond that of a Kaddish, as he not only left a permanent record but linked his entire identity with the *mitzvah* of memorialization. By renaming himself after the Kaddish prayer itself, George chose to become what he literally did during the Holocaust and became a Kaddish to Kovno's Jews, including the six million who perished.

Your eyes as well as mine bear witness to George as a Kaddish to all of Europe's Jews and his work as a living Kaddish. As viewers to George's photographs, we now have to fulfill our role. In some ways, we are a kind of Kaddish now and it is only by educating others about George's photographs that we will ensure that the dead will never be forgotten. As a Kaddish, we need to bear witness to not only George's photography but his life and death. The *mitzvah* George embodied is one we must fulfill. It is only by performing *mitzvah* that we can transform grief and suffering into justice (*tzedek*). As George performed his *mitzvah* by recording, we must fulfill ours by educating others about hate, intolerance, and racism. Teaching those about the existence of extraordinary humanity in the midst of unprecedented inhumanity is our only hope for justice in an unjust world.

We may become overwhelmed by the power of George's photographs and the commitment he epitomized but we must acknowledge two realities: we are not alone in this process of educating those around us and we are also not alone in mourning those that died. Fulfilling both *mitzvahs* of mourning the dead and making sure they are not forgotten are daunting responsibilities, ". . . to be a Kaddish is to be willing to suffer the grief of remembering." (138). Judaism acknowledges this burden and emphasizes support from others. In fact, receiving support during one's role as a Kaddish is a law. According to halachah [Jewish law], Kaddish is forbidden in the absence of community . . ." (139). "Thus, in order to say Kaddish, . . . mourners must stand with at least nine other Jews." (140). This quorum of people is called a *minyan* and the Jewish tradition requires at least ten Jewish men over the age of thirteen for the recitation of the Kaddish prayer.

I will never know if George intended to incorporate a sense of community and camaraderie in his photography but in considering his photography and viewers like us who have witnessed life in the Kovno ghetto through his camera lens, George has a symbolic *minyan* numbering in the thousands. Every visitor to the United States Holocaust Memorial Museum in Washington D.C., Simon Wiesenthal Center and Museum of Tolerance in Los Angeles, and Beth Hatefutsoth in Israel is a participant in George Kaddish's quorum. In a way, by seeing George's "Kaddish" of photography, we are saying Kaddish for those he photographed and with every new museum attendee, George's *minyan* in this post-Holocaust world grows. Within this ever-growing quorum is the shared honor and burden of bearing witness to the six million. This responsibility is just not extended to the family members or friends of those murdered but all of us who will educate others about what he saw. As viewers we are not linked by blood but by resistance. Just like George and those he photographed, we must keep the memory of humanity alive. Doing so will combat intolerance and hate. World War II is over but intolerance is still with us. Rabbi Bercovits in *Faith After the Holocaust* states, ". . . the Final Solution . . . is far from being final." (141).

Outside the context of the Holocaust and as mentioned before, the Kaddish also instructs Jews to praise God despite the loss of family and friends—as no event in life tests one's faith in God than the death of a loved one. Within the parameters of the Holocaust, there is an undeniable echo to this centuries old prayer: as no event in life tests one's faith in God more than the death of a loved one, no other event in modern human history tests the world's faith in humanity than the Holocaust. But we do have faith: George's images show that humanity existed during the Holocaust and still exists after it. As it is commanded that the Kaddish prayer be recited in order to praise God despite great, personal loss, George's Kaddish of photography needs to be seen and discussed because the humanity of the Jews needs to be equally praised despite the Holocaust. George was far from "meshuggeh;" the word accusing George of being crazy. On the contrary George knew that the Nazis would deny mass murder and he also knew that someone would be left behind, even after he died, to see his work and take on both the duty and privilege to remember and proclaim the Jews' resistance and dignity. Witnessing after the witness is the responsibility George bestows to us now. It is true; a journey of a thousand miles begins where one is standing. A long time ago, I once stood by George's unopened boxes of photographs. George's chronicle took me back to another time and place. George recorded the existence of grace and goodness in the midst of evil and now gives me and you the responsibility to tell others about the dangers of inequality and bigotry. In a larger sense, the lens of George's focus is not only on Kovno, Lithuania but our entire world. As the homeless on the street and *tzitzit* remind the Jew to obey God's laws and right human wrongs in the name of human rights, social injustice in places like China, the former Yugoslavia, Cambodia, Rwanda, Darfur, Tibet, Cuba and even on our own soil and elsewhere, remind us of our commitment to *tzedakah*. We are not alone but are with George in teaching others about the importance of human rights for all.

" . . . I have a dream today.

I have a dream that one day every valley shall be exalted, every hill and mountain shall be made low, and rough places will be made plains, and the crooked places will be made straight, and the glory of the Lord shall be revealed, and all flesh shall see it together.

This is our hope. This is the faith with which I return to the south. With this faith we will be able to hew out of the mountain of despair a stone of hope. With this faith we will be able to transform the jangling discords of our nation into a beautiful symphony of brotherhood. With this faith we will be able to work together, to pray together, to struggle together, to go to jail together, to stand up for freedom together, knowing that we will be free one day.

This will be the day when all of God's children will be able to sing with a new meaning "My country 'tis of thee, sweet land of liberty, of thee I sing. Land where my fathers died, land of the pilgrim's pride, from every mountainside, let freedom ring."

And if America is to be a great nation this must come true. So let freedom ring from the prodigious hilltops of New Hampshire. Let freedom ring from the mighty mountains of New York. Let freedom ring from the heightening Alleghenies of Pennsylvania.

Let freedom ring from the snowcapped Rockies of Colorado.

Let freedom ring from the curvaceous peaks of California.

But not only that—let freedom ring from Stone Mountain in Georgia.

Let freedom ring from Lookout Mountain of Tennessee.

Let freedom ring from every hill and molehill of Mississippi. From every mountainside, let freedom ring.

When we let freedom ring, when we let it ring from every village and every hamlet, from every state and every city, we will be able to speed up that day when all of God's children, black men and white men, Jews and gentiles, Protestants and Catholics, will be able to join hands and sing in the words of the old Negro spiritual,

"Free at last! Free at last! Thank God Almighty, we are free at last!"

—excerpt from "I Have a Dream," Martin Luther King Jr.
(28 August 1963)

Thanks . . .

Many might think a sentence or two just saying "Keep on writing" or "Don't give up" is important but it is. The following is a list of people who gave me words of encouragement:

Floyd and Edris Dade, Ted and Mohkeed Gong, Gloria Lyon, Agnes Lindhardt, George Sarlo, Janet Holmgren, Chana Bloch, Kenneth Harmon, Sean Simplicio, Brian Ashford, Erica Simmons, Nick Drummond, Griffin Decker, Lani Silver, Linda Kornett, John Martinez, Paul Diop, Jonathan Cohen, Itoro Ibia, Joan Poss, Mary Felstiner, Joe Glass and Doumo, Lalesh Nagy, Jim Landers, Congressman John Lewis, Joel Segal, Barbara J. Hamlett, Bobby Vassar, Nir Buras, Joe Holzer, Pola Ganor, Don Joy, Randy Jennings, Anna Kendall and Princess, Greg Foster, Najja Bracey, Constant Tra, Shelly Jennings, Albert Bedrosian, Ron Greenberg, Mike Russell, Evelyn Szelenyi, Therese, Carol Mink, Betty Carlson, Jesus Vargas, Marge Josephson, Sandy Zweifach, Rick Lehner, Chris Taylor, Peppi DeBiaso, John Boudreau, Rachelle Kassimir, Mandy Liu, Zibu Sibanda, Steve Rosenkrantz, Jeff Jahangiri, Steve Laymon, Sarah Martin, Clyde Conklin, Ken James, Briana Feinberg, Sofia Pezua, Joe Militano, Auntie Julie, Sarath Sochannam, and last but not least my Uncle Frank and firefighters Pat Evans ("Big Pat"), Tim Curley ("Curless"), and Glenn Renick ("Herc" a.k.a. "coffee cake").

Note

Dear Reader—

Dr. Michael Berenbaum in his book, *The Last Days* wrote, "It is five minutes to midnight in the lives of Holocaust survivors . . . " If we wait too long to ask questions and show them respect, we will be too late.

Mr. Kaddish died before I finished writing and so did four other survivors. I was and am too late to tell them what they mean to me. This is my regret.

Learning from Holocaust survivors is of utmost importance but also learning from those who survived Jim Crow laws and segregation or who survived atrocities in places like Cambodia or Tiananmen Square ("Heaven's Gate") is equally important. Past and current knowledge of intolerance is everywhere. Our sense of humanity and basic existence depend on learning from those who witnessed intolerance.

You don't have to be Jewish or religious to understand the importance of memory and human rights; you need only be human.

I would like to know about what you will soon learn from other survivors and our world's elders, please write me at: *CatherineLGong@aol.com*

—C

Recommended Reading

Faith After the Holocaust, Rabbi Eli Bercovits

The World Must Know by Michael Berenbaum

Saying Kaddish by Anita Diamant

Heroism and Bravery in Lithuania: 1941-1945 by Alex Faitelsohn

Light One Candle by Solly Ganor

Responsa from the Holocaust and *The Annihilation of Lithuanian Jewry* by Rabbi Ephraim Oshry

The Hidden History of the Kovno Ghetto by The United States Holocaust Memorial Museum

Night by Elie Wiesel

Thanks for reading!

Notes

1. Michael Berenbaum, *The World Must Know*, ed. Arnold Kramer (Canada: Little, Brown and Company, 1993), p. 92.
2. Fox Butterfield, *China, Alive in the Bitter Sea* (New York: Bantam, 1982), p. 13.
3. Anita Diamant, *Saying Kaddish* (New York: Shocken, 1998), pp. 11-12.
4. Ibid. p.17.
5. phone conversation with Dina Abramowitz; YIVO Institute of Jewish Research. New York, New York. Summer 1997.
6. Michael Berenbaum, *The World Must Know*, ed. Arnold Kramer (Canada: Little, Brown and Company, 1993), p. 100.
7. phone conversation with George Birman; residence. New York, New York. Summer 1997.
8. phone conversation with George Kaddish; residence. Hollywood, Florida. Summer 1997.
9. personal correspondence from Rabbi Abraham Cooper; Simon Wiesenthal Center and Museum of Tolerance. Los Angeles, California. December 24, 1997.
10. United States Holocaust Memorial Museum (USHMM), Photo Archives. Washington, D.C. George Kaddish collection, photo reference sheet #81073.
11. Solly Ganor, *Light One Candle* (New York: Kodansha International, 1995), p. 225. Reprinted by permission of Kodansha America, LLC. Excerpted from LIGHT ONE CANDLE by Solly Ganor published by Kodansha America, Inc. (1995).
12. United States Holocaust Memorial Museum (USHMM), Photo Archives. Washington, D.C. George Kaddish collection, photo reference sheet #15472.
13. Ibid.
14. Ibid.
15. Ibid.
16. Ibid.
17. Solly Ganor, *Light One Candle* (New York: Kodansha International, 1995), p. 226. Reprinted by permission of Kodansha America, LLC. Excerpted from LIGHT ONE CANDLE by Solly Ganor published by Kodansha America, Inc. (1995).

18. Ibid. p. 139. Reprinted by permission of Kodansha America, LLC. Excerpted from LIGHT ONE CANDLE by Solly Ganor published by Kodansha America, Inc. (1995).

19. Ibid. p. 248. Reprinted by permission of Kodansha America, LLC. Excerpted from LIGHT ONE CANDLE by Solly Ganor published by Kodansha America, Inc. (1995).

20. USHMM, *The Hidden History of the Kovno Ghetto* (Boston: Bullfinch Press, 1997), p. 55.

21. personal correspondence from Solly Ganor; Herzelia, Israel. November 15, 1998.

22. USHMM, *The Hidden History of the Kovno Ghetto,* (Boston: Bullfinch Press, 1997), p. 55.

23. personal correspondence from Solly Ganor. Herzelia, Israel. November 15, 1998.

24. United States Holocaust Memorial Museum (USHMM), Photo Archives. Washington, D.C. George Kaddish collection, photo reference sheet #09112A.

25. USHMM, *The Hidden History of the Kovno Ghetto* (Boston: Bullfinch Press, 1997), p. 217.

26. Solly Ganor, *Light One Candle* (New York: Kodansha International, 1995), p. 216. Reprinted by permission of Kodansha America, LLC. Excerpted from LIGHT ONE CANDLE by Solly Ganor published by Kodansha America, Inc. (1995).

27. personal correspondence from Solly Ganor. Herzelia, Israel. November 15, 1998.

28. United States Holocaust Memorial Museum (USHMM), Photo Archives. Washington, D.C. George Kaddish collection, photo reference sheet #10795.

29. Solly Ganor, *Light One Candle* (New York: Kodansha International, 1995), p. 99. Reprinted by permission of Kodansha America, LLC. Excerpted from LIGHT ONE CANDLE by Solly Ganor published by Kodansha America, Inc. (1995).

30. Ibid. p. 232. Reprinted by permission of Kodansha America, LLC. Excerpted from LIGHT ONE CANDLE by Solly Ganor published by Kodansha America, Inc. (1995).

31. Ibid. p. 246-8. Reprinted by permission of Kodansha America, LLC. Excerpted from LIGHT ONE CANDLE by Solly Ganor published by Kodansha America, Inc. (1995).

32. Ibid. p. 216-7 Reprinted by permission of Kodansha America, LLC. Excerpted from LIGHT ONE CANDLE by Solly Ganor published by Kodansha America, Inc. (1995).

33. Ibid. p. 217 Reprinted by permission of Kodansha America, LLC. Excerpted from LIGHT ONE CANDLE by Solly Ganor published by Kodansha America, Inc. (1995).

34. Ibid. pp. 221-2 Reprinted by permission of Kodansha America, LLC. Excerpted from LIGHT ONE CANDLE by Solly Ganor published by Kodansha America, Inc. (1995).

35. personal correspondence from Solly Ganor. Herzelia, Israel. November 15, 1998.

36. Solly Ganor, *Light One Candle* (New York: Kodansha International, 1995), pp. 56-7. Reprinted by permission of Kodansha America, LLC. Excerpted from LIGHT ONE CANDLE by Solly Ganor published by Kodansha America, Inc. (1995).

37. Ibid. pp. 57-8. Reprinted by permission of Kodansha America, LLC. Excerpted from LIGHT ONE CANDLE by Solly Ganor published by Kodansha America, Inc. (1995).

38. Solly Ganor, *Light One Candle* (New York: Kodansha International, 1995), p. 68. Reprinted by permission of Kodansha America, LLC. Excerpted from LIGHT ONE CANDLE by Solly Ganor published by Kodansha America, Inc. (1995).

39. USHMM, *The Hidden History of the Kovno Ghetto* (Boston: Bullfinch Press, 1997), p. 18.

40. Ibid. p. 19.

41. Ibid.

42. Solly Ganor, *Light One Candle* (New York: Kodansha International, 1995), p. 92. Reprinted by permission of Kodansha America, LLC. Excerpted from LIGHT ONE CANDLE by Solly Ganor published by Kodansha America, Inc. (1995).

43. Ibid. p. 87. Reprinted by permission of Kodansha America, LLC. Excerpted from LIGHT ONE CANDLE by Solly Ganor published by Kodansha America, Inc. (1995).

44. Ibid. p. 94. Reprinted by permission of Kodansha America, LLC. Excerpted from LIGHT ONE CANDLE by Solly Ganor published by Kodansha America, Inc. (1995).

45. Ibid. p. 194. Reprinted by permission of Kodansha America, LLC. Excerpted from LIGHT ONE CANDLE by Solly Ganor published by Kodansha America, Inc. (1995).

46. Ibid. p. 214. Reprinted by permission of Kodansha America, LLC. Excerpted from LIGHT ONE CANDLE by Solly Ganor published by Kodansha America, Inc. (1995).

47. Leib Garfunkel, "The Destruction of Kovno's Jewry," trans. and paraphrased by Alfred Katz (United States Holocaust Memorial Museum, Washington, D.C., 1995), 41.

48. Solly Ganor, *Light One Candle* (New York: Kodansha International, 1995), pp. 142-4. Reprinted by permission of Kodansha America, LLC. Excerpted from LIGHT ONE CANDLE by Solly Ganor published by Kodansha America, Inc. (1995).

49. Ibid. p. 145-6. Reprinted by permission of Kodansha America, LLC. Excerpted from LIGHT ONE CANDLE by Solly Ganor published by Kodansha America, Inc. (1995).

50. Ibid. p. 233. Reprinted by permission of Kodansha America, LLC. Excerpted from LIGHT ONE CANDLE by Solly Ganor published by Kodansha America, Inc. (1995).

51. Ibid.p. 235. Reprinted by permission of Kodansha America, LLC. Excerpted from LIGHT ONE CANDLE by Solly Ganor published by Kodansha America, Inc. (1995).

52. Ibid. p. 159. Reprinted by permission of Kodansha America, LLC. Excerpted from LIGHT ONE CANDLE by Solly Ganor published by Kodansha America, Inc. (1995).

53. Ibid. p. 161. Reprinted by permission of Kodansha America, LLC. Excerpted from LIGHT ONE CANDLE by Solly Ganor published by Kodansha America, Inc. (1995).

54. Ibid. p. 136. Reprinted by permission of Kodansha America, LLC. Excerpted from LIGHT ONE CANDLE by Solly Ganor published by Kodansha America, Inc. (1995).

55. Ibid. pp. 235-6. Reprinted by permission of Kodansha America, LLC. Excerpted from LIGHT ONE CANDLE by Solly Ganor published by Kodansha America, Inc. (1995).

56. Ibid. p. 137. Reprinted by permission of Kodansha America, LLC. Excerpted from LIGHT ONE CANDLE by Solly Ganor published by Kodansha America, Inc. (1995).

57. Ibid. p. 245. Reprinted by permission of Kodansha America, LLC. Excerpted from LIGHT ONE CANDLE by Solly Ganor published by Kodansha America, Inc. (1995).

58. Ibid. pp. 163-4. Reprinted by permission of Kodansha America, LLC. Excerpted from LIGHT ONE CANDLE by Solly Ganor published by Kodansha America, Inc. (1995).

59. United States Holocaust Memorial Museum (USHMM), Photo Archives. Washington, D.C. George Kaddish collection, photo reference sheet #81128.

60. USHMM, *The Hidden History of the Kovno Ghetto* (Boston: Bullfinch Press, 1997), p. 248.

61. Solly Ganor, *Light One Candle* (New York: Kodansha International, 1995), p. 259. Reprinted by permission of Kodansha America, LLC. Excerpted from LIGHT ONE CANDLE by Solly Ganor published by Kodansha America, Inc. (1995).

62. Michael Berenbaum, *The World Must Know*, ed. Arnold Kramer (Canada: Little, Brown and Company, 1993), p. 92.

63. Anita Diamant, *Saying Kaddish* (New York: Shocken, 1998), p. 11.

64. Ibid. p. 13.

65. Ibid. pp. 11-12

66. Ibid. p. 14.

67. Ibid. pp. 11-12.

68. Ibid. p. 15.

69. Ibid. pp. 62-4.

70. Jack Riemer, "Introduction: Jewish Insights on Death," in *Wrestling with the Angel*, ed. Jack Riemer (New York: Shocken, 1995), pp. 10-11.

71. Anita Diamant, *Saying Kaddish* (New York: Shocken, 1998), p. 70.
72. Leon Wieseltier, *Kaddish* (New York:Vintage, 1998), p. 314.
73. Ibid.
74. Anita Diamant, *Saying Kaddish* (New York: Shocken, 1998), pp. 23-4.
75. Leon Wieseltier, *Kaddish* (New York:Vintage, 1998), p. 314.
76. Anita Diamant, *Saying Kaddish* (New York: Shocken, 1998), p. 28.
77. Ibid. p. 23.
78. Patricia Barry, "On Being the Kaddish," in *Wrestling with the Angel*, ed. Jack Riemer (New York: Shocken, 1995), p.300.
79. Solly Ganor, *Light One Candle* (New York: Kodansha International, 1995), p. 259. Reprinted by permission of Kodansha America, LLC. Excerpted from LIGHT ONE CANDLE by Solly Ganor published by Kodansha America, Inc. (1995).
80. Ibid. p. 303. Reprinted by permission of Kodansha America, LLC. Excerpted from LIGHT ONE CANDLE by Solly Ganor published by Kodansha America, Inc. (1995).
81. Anita Diamant, *Saying Kaddish* (New York: Shocken, 1998), p. 24.
82. Solly Ganor, *Light One Candle* (New York: Kodansha International, 1995), p. 316. Reprinted by permission of Kodansha America, LLC. Excerpted from LIGHT ONE CANDLE by Solly Ganor published by Kodansha America, Inc. (1995).
83. Anita Diamant, *Saying Kaddish* (New York: Shocken, 1998), p. 34.
84. Elie Wiesel, *Night* (New York: Hill and Wang, 2006), p. 33.
85. Ibid.
86. Solly Ganor, *Light One Candle* (New York: Kodansha International, 1995), p. 167. Reprinted by permission of Kodansha America, LLC. Excerpted from LIGHT ONE CANDLE by Solly Ganor published by Kodansha America, Inc. (1995).
87. USHMM, *The Hidden History of the Kovno Ghetto*, (Boston: Bullfinch Press, 1997), p. 217.
88. Patricia Barry, "On Being the Kaddish," in *Wrestling with the Angel*, ed. Jack Riemer (New York: Shocken, 1995), p.300.
89. Ibid. p. 300.
90. Ibid.
91. Anita Diamant, *Saying Kaddish* (New York: Shocken, 1998), p. 14.
92. United States Holocaust Memorial Museum (USHMM), Photo Archives. Washington, D.C. George Kaddish collection, photo reference sheet #81128.
93. Rabbi Ephraim Oshry, *Responsa from the Holocaust* (New York: Judaica Press, 1989). p. 6.
94. USHMM, *The Hidden History of the Kovno Ghetto* (Boston: Bullfinch Press, 1997), p. 181.
95. United States Holocaust Memorial Museum (USHMM), Photo Archives. Washington, D.C. George Kaddish collection, photo reference sheet #10920.
96. Solly Ganor, *Light One Candle* (New York: Kodansha International, 1995), p. 207. Reprinted by permission of Kodansha America, LLC. Excerpted from

LIGHT ONE CANDLE by Solly Ganor published by Kodansha America, Inc. (1995).

97. Ibid. p. 210. Reprinted by permission of Kodansha America, LLC. Excerpted from LIGHT ONE CANDLE by Solly Ganor published by Kodansha America, Inc. (1995).

98. Ibid. p. 208. Reprinted by permission of Kodansha America, LLC. Excerpted from LIGHT ONE CANDLE by Solly Ganor published by Kodansha America, Inc. (1995).

99. Ibid. p. 139. Reprinted by permission of Kodansha America, LLC. Excerpted from LIGHT ONE CANDLE by Solly Ganor published by Kodansha America, Inc. (1995).

100. Eliezer Berkovits, *Faith After the Holocaust* (New York: KTAV Publishing House, Inc., 1973), p. 78.

101. Ibid. p. 78-9.

102. Ibid. p. 79.

103. Edward Feld, *The Spirit of Renewal: Finding Faith after the Holocaust* (Vermont: Jewish Lights Publishing, 1994), p. 112.

104. Ibid. p. 112.

105. Ibid.

106. Eliezer Berkovits, *Faith After the Holocaust* (New York: KTAV Publishing House, Inc., 1973), p. 80.

107. Giuliani Mossimo, *Theological Implications of the Shoah* (New York: Peter Lang Publishing, 2002), p. 126.

108. Ibid.

109. Rabbi Ted Falcon, *Judaism for Dummies* (New York: Hungry Minds, 2001), p. 45.

110. Ibid. p. 44.

111. Anita Diamant, *Saying Kaddish* (New York: Shocken, 1998), p. 167.

112. Rabbi Ted Falcon, *Judaism for Dummies* (New York: Hungry Minds, 2001), p. 46.

113. USHMM, *The Hidden History of the Kovno Ghetto* (Boston: Bullfinch Press, 1997), p. 106.

114. Ibid. p. 149.

115. Ibid. p. 184.

116. Ibid.

117. Rabbi Ted Falcon, *Judaism for Dummies* (New York: Hungry Minds, 2001), p. 45.

118. Ibid. p. 44.

119. Ibid. p. 45.

120. Ibid. p. 60.

121. Ibid. p. 61.

122. Rabbi Ephraim Oshry, *Responsa from the Holocaust* (New York: Judaica Press, 1989), p. 97.

123. Ibid.

124. Ibid. p. 98.

125. Bible, Numbers 15: 38-9.

126. Anita Diamant, *Saying Kaddish* (New York: Shocken, 1998), p. 37.

127. William W. Mishell, *Kaddish For Kovno* (Illinois: Chicago Review Press, Incorporated, 1998), p. 144.

128. Giuliani Mossimo, *Theological Implications of the Shoah* (New York: Peter Lang Publishing, 2002), p. 257.

129. Rabbi Ephraim Oshry, *Responsa from the Holocaust* (New York: Judaica Press, 1989), p. 24.

130. Anita Diamant, *Saying Kaddish* (New York: Shocken, 1998), p. 37.

131. Richard Bank, *The Everything Judaism Book* (Massachussetts: Adams Media Corporation, 2002), p. 219.

132. Rabbi Ephraim Oshry, *Responsa from the Holocaust* (New York: Judaica Press, 1989), p. 88.

133. Ibid.

134. Giuliani Mossimo, *Theological Implications of the Shoah* (New York: Peter Lang Publishing, 2002), p. 229.

135. Anita Diamant, *Saying Kaddish* (New York: Shocken, 1998), p. 13.

136. Agnes G. Herman, "Firepower in Mitzvot," in *Wrestling with the Angel*, ed. Jack Riemer (New York: Shocken, 1995), p. 308.

137. Patricia Z. Barry, "One Being the Kaddish," in *Wrestling with the Angel*, ed. Jack Riemer (New York: Shocken, 1995), p. 300.

138. Ibid. p. 301.

139. Anita Diamant, *Saying Kaddish* (New York: Shocken, 1998), p. 24.

140. Ibid. p. 8.

141. Eliezer Berkovits, *Faith After the Holocaust* (New York: KTAV Publishing House, Inc., 1973), p. 133.

Photography Credits and Notes

Page 16: United States Holocaust Memorial Museum (USHMM), Photo Archives. Washington, D.C. George Kaddish collection, photo reference sheet #04640.

Page 21: Ibid. #90228.

Page 32: Ibid. #81073.

Page 32: Ibid. #15430.

Page 33: Ibid. #15472.

Page 34: Ibid. #81072.

Page 35: Ibid. #81075.

Page 37: Ibid. #89237.

Page 38: Ibid. #09112A.

Page 40: Ibid. #25151.

Page 41: Ibid. #81176.

Page 42: Ibid. #10795.

Page 43: Ibid. #91034.

Page 44: Ibid. #10806.

Page 47: Ibid. #10697.

Page 48: Ibid. #37069.

Page 49: Ibid. #81095.

Page 50: By courtesy of Beth Hatefutsoth, Photo Archive, Zvi Kadushin collection, Tel Aviv.

Page 50: By courtesy of Beth Hatefutsoth, Photo Archive, Zvi Kadushin collection, Tel Aviv.

Page 51: By courtesy of Beth Hatefutsoth, Photo Archive, Zvi Kadushin collection, Tel Aviv.

Page 51: United States Holocaust Memorial Museum (USHMM), Photo Archives. Washington, D.C. George Kaddish collection, photo reference sheet #81094.

Page 52: Ibid. #55085.

Page 53: Ibid. #81064.

Page 53: Ibid. #90226.

Page 54: Ibid. #81068.

Page 55: Ibid. #50682.

Page 56: Ibid. #25146.

Page 57: Ibid. #81152.

Page 58: Ibid. #81153.

Page 59: Ibid. #25741 and cited information from photo archives ref. sheet #88939.

Page 60: United States Holocaust Memorial Museum (USHMM), Photo Archives. Washington, D.C. George Kaddish collection, photo reference sheet #10772.

Page 60: Ibid. #06546.

Page 61: Ibid. #06824.

Page 61: Ibid. #81142.

Page 62: Ibid. #10695.

Page 63: Ibid. #12421.

Page 63: Ibid. #27422A.

Page 64: Ibid. #81086.

Page 65: Ibid. #81081.

Page 66: Ibid. #81084.

Page 66: Ibid. #81093.

Page 67: Ibid. #81080.

Page 67: Ibid. #91007.

Page 68: Ibid. #81082.

Page 68: Ibid. #15508 and information from #81149.

Page 69: Ibid. #81128 and information from #81126.

Page 70: United States Holocaust Memorial Museum (USHMM), Photo Archives. Washington, D.C. George Kaddish collection, photo reference sheet #37884.

Page 71: Ibid. #81129.

Page 71: Ibid. #81126.

Page 72: Ibid. #81123.

Page 86: Ibid. #81172.

Page 87: Ibid. #81178.

Page 87: Ibid. #81154.

Page 88: Ibid. #10920.

Page 89: Ibid. #91046.

Page 89: Ibid. #15433.

Page 90: Ibid. #90211.

Page 94: Ibid. #39069.

Page 97: Ibid. #15505.

Page 98: Ibid. #81175.

Page 102: Ibid. 80977.